GOD'S THOUSAND WAYS
THE STORY OF
ONE PERSON'S STRUGGLE FOR SURVIVAL

"Our heavenly Father has a thousand ways to provide for us of which we know nothing."—Ellen G. White, *The Ministry of Healing*, p. 481.

This is Jean Andrew's life - Jean is Joy Blitsche's sister. Jean Andrews is the real author - She used another name to protect the family.

GOD'S THOUSAND WAYS

THE STORY OF
ONE PERSON'S STRUGGLE FOR SURVIVAL

JOAN RICHARDS

Review and Herald Publishing Association
Washington, D.C.

This book was
Edited by Gerald Wheeler
Designed by Robert Wright
Cover Photograph by Robert Wright
Type set: 11/12 Corona

Printed in U.S.A.

Richards, Joan
    Survival

    I. Title.
            286.73 [B]

ISBN 0-8280-0101-4

TABLE OF CONTENTS

Chapter 1

The Break

The click of the door seemed unnaturally loud, maybe because Joan Richards was hearing more than just the door of the hospital room shutting. She was listening to the sound of her life closing to happiness. That door locked her husband of thirteen years into the psychiatric ward of Plains General Hospital.

Blinded by tears, she stumbled to the car to drive back to her sister's. Though Joan seldom took any medications, her sister Laurie insisted she swallow a tranquilizer so she could get some sleep. Laurie knew she had not slept well for some weeks, ever since Tim's latest siege of depression had begun.

Joan had become used to his twice-yearly bout with depression and usually managed to take it in stride fairly well, but this time was different. Usually he would miss a few days of teaching, using the excuse that he had the flu, and then as his depression lifted a little, he would once again cope with his daily routine.

But this fall the depression refused to vanish as usual. He consulted with Dr. Masters, who prescribed the usual tranquilizers, but to no avail. The depression seemed determined to stay.

He made an appointment to see a psychologist, but after taking the diagnostic tests he refused to return. He felt the psychologist might see too much of what was inside his mind—and he couldn't face that.

When he went back to his physician, Dr. Masters decided to put him in the hospital for more extensive testing. When all the results came in, the physician decided Tim had low blood sugar. "You'll have to stick to a fairly strict diet," he explained. "If you control your diet your emotions should be more stable, too."

But talking with Joan privately, Masters expressed the opinion that, even though the tests had singled out low blood sugar as one cause of her husband's problem, Tim should go back to the psychologist. The doctor felt that some rather serious emotional problems also accompanied the blood-sugar difficulty.

"But Tim refuses to see the psychologist again," Joan said.

"Then we'll just have to do the best we can," the doctor sighed. "Perhaps the diet will help enough to pull his problem back down to size."

Both Joan and Tim hoped that his terrible depressions might become a thing of the past. They shopped for high-protein foods and snacks for him to eat between meals. If they could only keep the blood sugar up consistently, perhaps his moods could stay up too.

But the depression hung on. "I might as well be dead! I'm no good to you or the kids this way," Tim moaned. Moaned repeatedly to himself.

"But I love you!" Joan argued back. "I want you alive, not dead. I'm sure you won't always feel this way. Your depression will go away as it always has."

Night after unending night they spent arguing the respective roles they had slipped into. Finally Joan would end the discussion by pretending to fall asleep. Long after his even breathing told her he was sleeping, she would stop trembling enough to get an hour or two of rest.

During the day she had to go to her job as usual. Tim was too depressed to teach, so she left 4-year-old Mark with him and took the other children to school before going on to work herself. Then each evening the cycle began all over.

About a week after the onset of his extreme depression he decided he would try to teach again. He managed to make it through the first day, but the second day things began to fall apart and he returned home.

When Joan arrived that evening, she found an extremely upset husband. "I don't know how I got home," he told her, his hands shaking. "As I was driving, suddenly I realized I couldn't remember half the trip home. My mind had gone completely blank."

"Perhaps you were just thinking of something else." She hoped there was some kind of simple explanation.

"No, I know it's not that kind of thing. Sometimes the same thing happens to me at school. I'll be helping kids and realize all of a sudden that half an hour or even an hour has gone by without my knowing anything about what I've been doing."

In desperation Joan made an appointment for him to see a Christian psychiatrist. The doctor talked with him and prescribed some mood-elevating medication.

Again depression won the battle. It almost seemed that Tim fought against getting better. She knew he really wanted to have a happy, successful Christian life, yet depression had a hypnotic hold over him.

One morning Tim was totally frantic. "Tie me up! I'm afraid I'm going to hurt someone. Tie me up!"

In order to pacify him, Joan finally did as he asked, though she made such a clumsy job of it any child could have gotten free. That particular day Tim felt safe and managed to calm down, only because he was bound.

One day he insisted he needed to talk with the local educational superintendent and asked his wife to call him. That morning Tim had been so afraid to be left alone that she contacted her employer and told him she could not come to work. Now she telephoned the superintendent and asked whether he could come over and see her husband.

When Dr. Willerton entered the room, she noticed his shock at her husband's condition. Tim was where he would remain all day—in his reclining chair, with a blanket covering his six-foot frame. His usually ruddy cheeks were sallow, his head lolled to the side, and his voice was so weak it was difficult to understand him.

But what arrested the educational leader's attention was Tim's gaze. His blue-green eyes held a tortured look no human being should ever have.

Dr. Willerton encouraged Tim to seek whatever

help he needed to get back on his feet again, and then had prayer with him before leaving.

A few days later the family decided to visit Joan's sister Laurie. Joan hoped traveling might perk her husband up, but once they arrived at her sister's, he seemed to sink even lower. Worried, Laurie finally phoned her family doctor, who suggested they bring Tim in to the hospital for some tests.

Four days later the blow fell. The physician committed him to the psychiatric ward.

"Oh, God," Joan sobbed, "what am I going to do? It's more than I can stand."

Gradually, as she prayed, God helped her to know that He would never allow anything to come to her that was too great for the two of them to carry together.

The doctor sounded encouraging. "I think Tim's problem is comparatively simple. We'll give him some medication that will get him back on his feet and teaching within two to four weeks. In fact, he should be better than ever."

"Can you really make progress that fast?" Joan questioned, unable to believe a long nightmare could end so quickly.

"If there are no other complications," he explained, "this particular problem is actually quite easy to solve."

Although she didn't like that "if" part, she was so eager to see Tim well that she refused to think of any other possibility.

On Sunday, Joan had to return home to get the children back to school and continue with her job. Having to limit her visits to the hospital to weekends, she drove the hundred-odd miles one way on

Friday afternoons and then made the return trip on Sundays.

Two weeks later the doctor asked to speak with her. "I'm afraid Tim's problem is deeper set and more complicated than I had thought. He's not responding to treatment as I had hoped. We will continue to work with him here before releasing him. But when he is released, where do you want us to send him?"

"Won't he be able to come home?"

Eager to have her husband back home and well, Joan could hardly believe there was any other choice.

"I think not. He really is in no shape to return home. In fact, in his present condition I believe it would be dangerous to the family to have him there."

Tears flowing, Joan bowed her head.

"Further," the doctor continued relentlessly, "he should remain in this area so we can follow through with treatment. If he is consistent with his medication, and if he will cooperate in his own recovery, I still believe we can get him back on his feet. It may take two years of careful supervision, but others have made it."

She could only nod her head, unable to ask all the questions she had.

"By the way, how is your financial situation?"

"Not good at all," she choked out. "Even with both of us working, we have to be awfully careful. I don't know all the details, for Tim has always paid the bills, but from what I see now, I may have to declare bankruptcy."

The doctor nodded. "I wondered about that. Tim told me everything was great, but I've seen people before who were ill as he is. One fellow I know went out and bought a house, a yacht, and a car all in one day—with fifty dollars in his pocket. That's the usual financial pattern for this type of illness."

Her thoughts churned in turmoil as she left his office that day. She didn't want Tim to know the verdict she had just received, so she tried to put on a smile for the short time she would have with him.

As she drove back to her sister's later, her mind wasn't on her driving. She blinked the tears away to see a van right in front of her. There was no way to avoid hitting it, but since she wasn't going fast, no one was hurt, and the damage to the vehicles was slight.

But with the rest of her world falling apart, the accident offered a good excuse to burst into tears. She could barely give the man the necessary information.

"If things are that bad, you shouldn't be driving at all," the other driver said angrily.

He was probably right, but each day she could only do what had to be done. She dared not stop for fear she would never start again.

Driving home that Sunday, Joan thought of the doctor's advice. How could she tell her husband he couldn't come home? She loved him and wanted to help him in any way she could. The tears started to fall, until finally she pulled over in a rest area to let the children run around.

While they played, Joan struggled with her feelings. A separation from the one she had promised to hold in sickness and in health was the last thing she wanted. Tears released some of her pent-up emotions, and she was able to start the car and resume the trip home.

Tim's father phoned to say he would come to see whether he could help. Though there really was nothing he could do, he did visit with his son. Joan appreciated his attitude tremendously. She knew of others in similar situations who did not receive such support from their in-laws.

Each morning she had to leave him at six-thirty to drive the children to school. Then she turned around to make the sixty-minute trip to work. In the afternoon the children stayed with various friends near the school until she could pick them up at six o'clock. Finally they would all arrive home at six-thirty.

Because Joan knew she could not continue such a schedule much longer, she prayed in a way she had never prayed before. "God, I need help. I can't continue this long-day schedule. Please send me help *by Monday.*"

Is it OK to give God a deadline? she wondered. She had always thought a person should ask for the things he needed and then trust Him to grant the requests at the best moment.

But in her desperation she told God she needed help by Monday. As usual she took the children to school early so she could get to work on time. During the day she called several people, both pastors and others, who might know of someone who could assist. No one did. In fact, she couldn't even find anyone to keep the children after school. She would have to leave work by two-thirty to get them.

Then about two o'clock the phone in her office rang. Her minister was on the line.

"Oh, pastor," Joan exclaimed, "I've tried to call

you several times today, but couldn't get you."

As she explained her need, he asked, "Have you checked with Mary Edwards? You know she lives near you, and her daughter attends the same school your children do."

"Really? No, I haven't. I don't think I know her."

"Well, I know where she works, so I'll check for you. I'm sure she will help you."

A few minutes later he phoned back, almost more thrilled than Joan was. "She'll do it!" he shouted. "If you can drop the kids off at her place in the morning, she'll take them to school. Then she'll pick them up after school and keep them until you get home from work. And she won't charge you anything. She says she'll be happy to do it all school year for you if you need it."

The words "If God be for us, who can be against us?" (Rom. 8:31) flashed through her mind. God was already showing her that the two of them together could carry even this burden. In spite of all the pressures on her, Joan felt the thrill of knowing His presence in her life.

Now the doctor warned her that she must never leave Tim alone with any of the children, not even for five minutes. "You can never know what shape he is really in," he explained. "He can seem fine one minute, and the next he may fall apart."

As she drove home Joan's thoughts kept returning to the question Why? There didn't seem to be any answer. She knew she had tried to help and encourage Tim during their marriage in every way she could, but still he had shattered. Her mind wandered back over their lives together. Was the answer there? Or did the problem come from childhood?

Chapter 2

Roots

"TIM'S CONDITION CRITICAL STOP MULTI-PLE BEE STINGS STOP PLEASE COME IMMEDI-ATELY STOP"

Mr. Richards' voice shook as he read the tele-gram. "Condition critical! What under the sun has happened?"

"I knew we should never have sent him so far from home to go to school," his wife moaned. "We should have kept him with us somehow, even if I had to teach him myself!"

"Now, Ellen," her husband comforted, "acci-dents happen wherever we are. You know you couldn't teach him and work, too."

"But surely we could have done something differently! Let me go pack. We want to catch the first plane out."

"Can we both manage to go? Linda's been so sick lately I'd hate to have you leave her."

"That's right! I guess I'll have to stay with the younger children and let you go alone to Tim." She began to cry, unable to accept the idea that her firstborn son might be dying and she couldn't go to him. Why had they ever come to this place, anyway?

When Tim was 6 and his brother, Carl, 2, the family had left the United States to come to Africa as missionaries. Linda was born two years later. Because their part of the country had no adequate schools, Tim had had to stay with another missionary family many miles from home in order to attend one.

For Tim's 10th birthday his "foster family" planned a picnic. Taking his birthday cake along with their lunch, they climbed a small hill out in the wilds of Africa. As the children played before lunch, Tim challenged the others to a race. As they sped down the hill, one of them accidentally kicked over a beehive.

For some reason known only to bees, they decided Tim was the one who had done the terrible thing. Every one of the insects concentrated single-mindedly on him, ignoring all the other children.

Tim received more than five hundred bee stings over his body. In the hospital his foster mother asked, "Do you want to give a message to your parents?" The boy realized she didn't expect him to live to see them again.

When Mr. Richards arrived, he could not hide his shock at his son's condition. Immediately he covered his feelings, but the damage was already done.

"Am I going to die, Dad?" Tim asked in fright.

"Of course not, son. You're only sore from so many bee stings."

But Tim knew it was serious. He determined that day that he would live. Within a few days he was able to leave the hospital to make the trip home. A week after his release his father pulled more than three hundred stingers from the boy's chest alone.

Thrilled to be home again, Tim greeted all his special places, especially the big tree out in back of the house. He had spent many happy hours hidden in its foliage. Now he wrestled with his 6-year-old brother and tickled his baby sister. Then he ran to throw his arms around his diminutive mother. Already he was almost as tall as she, but that wasn't saying much, since she was barely five feet. She had taught him the songs of Jesus and talked often of His love and care. Tim had learned early that her patience and humor could weather any situation.

For their vacation that year the family decided to travel through some of Africa's wild beauty. However, the roads did not quite come up to the standards their car was used to.

Just at dusk the children became frightened when they again got stuck in the mud. Father hauled out the shovel to dig them out for the umpteenth time that day.

While he worked, mother began an impromptu concert. Thousands of people had enjoyed her voice and musicianship on both piano and organ as she worked with her evangelist husband over the years. Now she became a composer, as well. Her old college song formed the basis for her new composition:

> We sling-a de mud
> And push-a de car along.

The children forgot their fear as they laughed and sang along with her.

When Tim was 12, the family transferred from Africa to Singapore. A dream come true for Tim, he spent every free minute on his bike or in the swimming pool. In Singapore he could live at home and attend school nearby.

Three years later the first shadow fell across his young life. His father underwent emergency cancer surgery.

"You'd better return to the States, where you can receive better medical care than you can here," the doctor advised. "I think we got it all, but with cancer you never know."

The family traveled to the States. At first they bounced from one side of the country to the other as the father tried to find a job, but finally they settled in a large city. Tim's mother secured a good position in the area, and life calmed down again.

About a year later Mr. Richards accepted a teaching assignment at a college some miles away. He took the boys with him, while his wife and daughter stayed in the city. Ellen had promised when she obtained her job that she would stay at least a year, and she still had a few months to go. She planned to join the family as soon as she could.

Meantime her husband bought a house so the family could have a permanent home. When the time came for Ellen and Linda to join the male half of the family, they discovered that the apartment lease stood in the way. They would have to wait another few months.

During this time the family drifted apart. No one made any conscious decision to separate, and they visited back and forth often, but a new independence came to each. The day came when they chose to separate permanently. The damage cancer had failed to do to the family, isolation accomplished easily.

For 17-year-old Tim it was an unbelievable nightmare. He simply couldn't handle the emotional coldness of the two people he loved most in all the world. Barely into a new school year, he dropped out for several months. He got a job teaching in an emergency situation, but after a few weeks his depression grew so dark he could not continue. All he wanted to do was go to bed and pull the covers over his head.

Alarmed, his father took him to his mother, who made an appointment with a neurologist. Under his care the depression finally lifted, and the next academic year found Tim back in school and doing well.

Joan's background seemed on the surface to be fairly similar to Tim's. They both grew up in the same denomination. Her father was a teacher and lay preacher, while Tim's father was a minister turned teacher. Both homes had similar income levels. The one major difference she could see was that her family had remained together in close Christian love.

Right after Joan's birth, her mother had to return to work to supplement the family income and left the girl in the care of a neighbor woman who had no children of her own. Perhaps because she could not have any herself, Frances loved and cared for the child as her own.

Though Frances' husband was a fine Christian man, she herself had no interest in religion. She liked her cigarettes and felt no need to change her life.

But smoke around Baby Joan? Never! Afraid to leave her small charge even for a moment, Frances did without smoking all day. At last she decided she might as well stop altogether. Still she wasn't about to get caught in any Christianity. In order to escape the pressures of her own conscience, she decided to leave her husband and return home to her mother.

However, it did not bring the peace she thought it would. Who is taking care of Joan? she constantly worried. Does the baby sitter love her as much as I do?

Unable to stand being separated from the infant she loved, Frances returned to her husband. She had used her last ounce of resistance in leaving him. Now her stubborn heart melted as she again cared for the child. Frances determined to dedicate her entire life to God's service. Never again would she attempt to run from Him.

Joan lived a happy, carefree life in the rural community where her parents had settled. With her parents, older sister—and Frances—she had a full and happy childhood. Later she recalled many hours of playing in the little stream that ran through their property. Fortunately her mother had the patience to put up with all the jars of polliwogs and insects Joan brought home.

The move to the city when the girl was 7 was exciting. For one thing, she would finally get to start school. Test results indicated she could handle more advanced work than first grade, so her first year in school was the fourth grade. Although capable of doing the classwork, the girl lagged socially. Gradually through the years she caught up and learned to make and keep friends.

The summer Joan received an invitation to go on a vacation to the beach with a friend was a high point for her. Lazy days spent playing in the surf with Melissa and her older brother gave Joan a tanned and healthy look her fair skin seldom had.

One day Melissa's brother towed both girls out into the surf on a rubber raft. Suddenly a wave upset them, sending them tumbling into deep water. While Joan could swim, the ocean was something else again. Melissa immediately crawled back on the raft, but when Joan came up she found herself directly under the raft—with the other girl on top. Instinctively Joan grabbed for the one solid thing around, only to find herself still under water, hanging on with both hands to the raft above her head.

Meanwhile Melissa and her brother became frantic. The boy decided to tow his sister to shore before returning to search for the other girl.

Joan never remembered getting out of the water. One minute she was trapped under the raft, the next she lay on the beach. She felt her guardian angel had been busy that day.

One summer her father had to travel some distance to attend school. For some reason the girl never understood, the money he thought was coming to her mother never arrived. Joan's mother didn't want him to drop his classes to come home because of it, so she wouldn't tell him the family had a problem.

Since they rented from the school where her dad taught, they at least had a roof over their heads. But what about food? And what about music lessons, which to them were almost as necessary?

Mother called the children together. "Kids, in Psalm 146:7 God has promised that He 'giveth food to the hungry.' Let's pray that He will send us enough money for food today."

Together they knelt while each one prayed, beginning with mother, then Laurie, Joan, and the youngest, Lynn. "Dear Jesus, please send us enough money to buy food for today."

Then they searched the house. They checked down in the couch, behind the piano, under the throw rug—all the usual places where money likes to hide.

Each day they found just enough to buy another loaf of bread and a quart of milk. Not once did they go hungry. Nor did they even have to skip a music lesson.

Joan learned that summer that not only does God keep His promises, He also has a sense of humor. The angels must have had a marvelous time day after day deciding where to hide the money.

Toward the end of the summer Laurie got a job that brought in enough money to help. The girls gave their father an especially warm welcome at the end of that summer. Life seemed a little easier with the head of the family home again.

As Joan entered her teens she found depression becoming a way of life for her. Nothing on the outside seemed wrong. She liked school, her family was close—but depression had a stranglehold on her that, try as she would, she could not break.

In college she worked for a wonderful Christian man who was like a second father to her, but nothing could lift the blackness of her emotions. She saw all her days as shades of gray. Color and brightness could not penetrate the wall of darkness surrounding her.

Then something happened to make her feel even worse. The man she worked for became ill with cancer. In fact, the doctor said he had only a few weeks to live. Not wanting the other teachers or students to know, because he couldn't have taken their pity and sympathy, he told only his wife, the college president, and Joan, his secretary.

"I can't stand it," Joan sobbed to herself. "Oh, God, why Prof? He loves You, and his wife and four children need him. You know his little girl is only 3. You can't let her grow up without a father!"

Joan had understood God's existence, power, and even humor before, but now for the first time she came to understand His love. The Lord performed two miracles that year. The teacher lived free of cancer for sixteen years before it recurred. When he died two years after becoming ill again, his youngest child was 21 instead of 3.

But the bigger miracle happened to Joan. She discovered for herself that God really cares. Of course, Satan had no intention of letting her go that easily. He knew the power depression had over her and attempted to use it to break her newfound relationship with God.

When a boy she was dating broke up with her just a few weeks later, she plunged again into the emotional depths. But this time it frightened her. Realizing its power, she turned immediately to her new Friend. "Lord," she prayed aloud, "I need You. I don't know why Dave broke up with me, but please help me."

She found that if she prayed out loud within an hour after the emotional letdown first hit, God would lift the darkness immediately. If she waited, the blackness would close it, making it much more difficult to reach out to Him.

Now color and brightness filled her life. She no longer saw the days as dull-gray to black, for the light of God's love overflowed in her heart.

Chapter 3

Rose-colored Glasses

I won't get involved, she stormed silently. No matter who he is or how cute he is, I'm not about to get hurt again.

Joan should have known better than to go with Brian in the first place. They had been casual friends for some time before he asked for help with a correspondence course in English grammar he was taking.

Since it was a subject she understood fairly well, she agreed to tutor him. The first time he came to her house they worked on the lessons together. Brian then left the rest of the course with her after making an appointment to come back in a week.

But when he returned, he expressed surprise that she had not done any of his lessons for him.

"I can't do that," she protested. "It wouldn't be honest. I'll *help* you with the lessons, but I won't do them for you."

"OK. That's fine," he agreed. "Would you like to go to the Amateur Hour with me next Saturday night?"

"I'd love to."

He took the lessons with him when he left that

day. Later he told Joan that he had given them to someone willing to do them for him for a price.

But she excused him, deciding that somehow she must have misunderstood. Surely such a wonderful guy couldn't be dishonest. The whole world took on the brilliant hues of love.

However, a friend of Brian's family told her, "I would fall in love with the parents much faster than I would the son." Joan couldn't understand that. She loved his parents deeply—but *more* than Brian? Never!

As the weeks and months went by, her feelings grew until she could think of nothing but him. When he asked her to marry him Joan was so happy she thought she would burst. She could never have imagined having such a wonderful person for a husband.

Then his work took him to another part of the country. The letters flew back and forth several times a week as the courtship grew even warmer by mail than it had in person. They made wedding plans for the following summer, even choosing the maid of honor and the best man.

But in the spring, when a young man's fancy supposedly turns *towards* thoughts of love, Brian's letters stopped coming. Finally, two weeks later, Joan received a note telling her he didn't want to marry her after all. Although he still professed his love for her, he never gave her any reason for breaking the engagement.

Joan was heartbroken. She had loved Brian with all her being, and the hurt went deep.

"Lord," she prayed, "You've said that true love is a gift from You. I don't believe You'd give half a gift by giving me love for Brian, but not giving him love for me. Either change his mind—or change me. It can't be Your will for me to go through life carrying a love that isn't from You. Please take care of it, Lord."

After putting her heart's affairs into the hands of the only One who could handle them, she felt better. Then she flew to a college three thousand miles from Brian, hoping that distance would make it easier to forget her heartbreak. And she determined not to allow anyone else to penetrate her defenses enough to hurt her.

When she dated Dale she liked him, but succeeded in remaining totally uninvolved. Dale, however, began to show signs of being seriously interested in her.

Then one of her teachers passed on some interesting gossip. "I hear Tim Richards is planning to ask you out."

"Who's Tim Richards? And how did you hear about it?" The efficiency of the local grapevine amused Joan.

"I have my ways," the woman chuckled. "Tim's the son of one of the teachers here. He's really a pretty nice guy, I think, but be careful! He has a reputation for being a heartbreaker."

Joan determined to be doubly on guard. She was willing to let him fall for her, but she intended to keep her own emotions free and unattached until she was 100 percent sure she would not get hurt.

As usual when someone asked her out—or even thought of doing so—Joan checked him out at the registrar's office where she worked. She didn't find out a lot of information, but age and GPA did tell her something. Although she wasn't a snob, she did like to learn what she could about a guy.

Tim asked her out right on schedule. She liked his dark good looks and ruddy cheeks, his sparkling eyes and tall slimness. Naturally, she decided he was cute. Joan was also impressed by a GPA that showed intelligence.

Remember, she told herself sternly, you're not going to fall for another heartbreaker!

Though she was not going steady with Dale, she still ended up having to break up with him. The hurt she saw in his eyes when she told him she could not continue dating him tore her up inside. Even her plan not to get involved did not protect her from pain. She discovered that the greatest agony was seeing someone else hurt.

As Joan and Tim began dating, however, no matter what she told herself, she began to fall in love again. Although her eyes were open a little more than they had been with Brian, the rose-colored glasses of emotion again made it hard to see anything less than perfection.

Then came the Christmas banquet. Tim gave her a single red rose to wear on her long white dress with the little red bows embroidered on it. The huge snowflakes falling softly against a backdrop of campus lights accentuated the romance of the evening. Her heart surrendered as Tim quietly asked her whether she would marry him.

Thinking momentarily of previous heartbreaks, she hesitated. Looking down at her rose, she thought its beauty seemed only to reflect the perfection she saw in Tim. "Let me think about it and pray about it first," she requested.

That night Joan went to the little prayer room in

the dorm to talk with her best Friend. "Lord, what should I do?" she asked.

The answer came instantly, as clearly as though Someone had spoken aloud. "You are to marry him. One of you will not live too long and there will be sorrow, but you are to marry him."

She couldn't believe what she had received. Surely there must be some mistake! Although she pleaded with God for guidance, the only answer was the same message repeated again. Returning to her room, she continued to hear the same words echoing and reechoing in the stillness of the night.

The next morning, in spite of all her intentions *not* to give Tim an answer so soon, she told him Yes. They began planning for an August wedding, since Tim needed to attend summer school to make up for having dropped out for a time several years before.

One of Tim's teachers drew her aside. "Because of his insecurity," the faculty member cautioned her, "I believe you will have to prove you love Tim over and over again. He's a fine boy, and it will be worth the effort, but he will need constant reassurance."

Confident her love would prove a complete cure for Tim's problem, she assured the professor that she wouldn't mind demonstrating her love for Tim forever.

The couple often went to his home, where Joan learned to love his father deeply. The heartache she detected there made her sympathetic toward each member of the family.

When the two of them visited Tim's mother and sister, Joan discovered that heartache is a two-way street. No one had benefited from the family's separation. Only hurt resulted. His mother had a sparkling personality that made everyone love her. But the sorrow Joan detected underlying even the good times wrenched the girl's heart.

One evening when Tim came over to the dorm to see her, his usual high good spirits seemed to have vanished.

"What's the matter, honey?" she asked.

"I don't know," he moaned.

"Surely something has happened. You don't just feel down for no reason."

"I just wish my folks were back together," he said, his voice shaking with emotion.

"I don't blame you, but you can't change them. What do you do to help yourself when you feel down?" Naively Joan felt that, since she had learned what to do for herself, surely he would also have discovered the secret of conquering depression.

"Nothing really. I always used to be totally happy, but since my folks have been apart, I'm miserable. Why can't they get back together?"

Joan thought a moment, then said positively, "God can give you the strength to survive no matter what your folks decide. All you need to do is put the whole problem in His hands. He can keep *you* from going down, regardless of what anyone else may do."

He shook his head. "I can't pray about it. How can people ask God to take care of the mess they make themselves?"

His reaction surprised her. "Why, God is just waiting for us to ask Him so He can make sense out of our confusion."

"Well, I can't pray about it."

Finally, at her insistence, they prayed together

over the problem, and Tim returned home. Within a day or two his spirits lifted.

Once again her rose-colored glasses helped her to dismiss the entire incident as unimportant.

After all, she thought, if Tim does have a problem with depression, surely I can help him, since I have learned to conquer it myself.

August finally came. They flew across the country to Joan's home, where they were to be married. His family would be there, together for the first time in months. But it was a painful situation, for his parents had postponed their divorce only because of the wedding.

As Joan walked down the aisle on her father's arm, her bridal bouquet of white stephanotis almost covering a small white Bible indicated a little of her dreams for a happy Christian home. Brian's mother, who still loved Joan as a daughter even though she was not marrying her son, had made the bridesmaids' dresses. Joan had discovered that the friend who had said she'd fall for the parents rather than the son was right.

Tim's father performed the ceremony, uniting the couple as husband and wife "for better or worse, in sickness and in health, until death do you part."

When it was over, Tim and Joan escaped for a short honeymoon at the beach. Soon they traveled to the small town in another State where he had been hired to teach in a little one-room school. They had rented a house right beside a beautiful lake, and they had each other. Walks together beside the sparkling lake among the brilliant fall leaves gave promise of even greater happiness to come. Life was especially beautiful when viewed through the perspective of two pairs of rose-colored glasses.

The newlyweds had been in their new home only two days when "their" first child arrived. Twelve-year-old Ronelle would be living in the pastor's home for the school year, but since the family would be gone for the first month of school, she would stay with the Richards at first.

Tim and Joan both loved children, so they were happy to help. Being "parents" after only two weeks of marriage did seem a little odd, but they joked and made a good time of the whole experience.

What the couple had failed to plan for was enough money to support their beautiful house. They simply couldn't manage to stay there and had to find a small apartment that they could afford.

Their second home was in an attractive setting on a small peninsula jutting out into a river—but it consisted of two rooms in someone else's house. By the time they moved a short time after school started, Joan was violently ill, so Tim had to do most of the packing. Also, she knew she would miss her privacy. Having to go through the landlord's house to get to their apartment seemed to dampen the fun the couple had been enjoying. Besides, the "flu" didn't subside as she expected it to. Finally she saw a doctor.

"Well," he told her, "it looks as though you're pregnant. But it appears to be complicated by a kidney infection. I'll give you some medication for the infection."

"Can you give me anything for the nausea, too?" she pleaded.

"I'm sure when your kidney infection clears up, your nausea will subside as well."

Unfortunately, it increased dramatically until she could barely get out of bed. When she called him, he said, "I think perhaps you'd better come into the hospital for a cystoscopy. That kidney infection should be clearing up by now."

Since she didn't know what a cystoscopy was, she decided to do what she always did when in doubt about a medical problem—call her uncle who was a doctor. "Uncle Rudy, what is a cystoscopy, anyway?"

"It's a kind of minor surgery in which the doctor inserts an instrument so he can actually see the kidneys."

"Is it safe to have this done during pregnancy?" she asked, concerned about her baby.

"It should be, but I'd do it only as a last resort. What kind of medication did the doctor give you?"

When she told him, he shouted, "But you're allergic to that!"

"I told him that," she explained, "but he said this kind could be safely taken, even though I react to other forms."

"Well, it can't," he stated bluntly. "What did your urinalysis show?"

"He didn't take one."

"What? He's planning to do a cystoscopy on a pregnant woman without even taking a urinalysis?" Joan thought the phone would explode long distance from his anger. "You stay away from him! He's dangerous and is only trying to fill the hospital."

Hanging up, Joan went to the bedroom to tell Tim. He had become ill that day and was not able to teach. She didn't understand yet what was happening as the first of many depressions shook him physically, mentally, and spiritually.

"I'm a failure. I'm going to quit," he cried.

"You can't fail until you quit," she rejoined. "If you keep on trying, no one can call you a failure. You've got to keep fighting to make it."

"I should be dead. I don't want to live!"

"Let's give the problem to God," she pleaded.

"God won't help me with problems I caused myself."

"Of course He will. He doesn't care what we did in the past. The Lord wants only to make our future better. He'll help you if you let Him."

"Then why aren't you perfect?" he snapped. "I see you reading your Bible and praying and I don't see God doing a lot for you."

"Please don't blame God for my mistakes," she said, almost in tears. "Without Him I'd be nothing."

"When I see God making you better, maybe then I'll believe He can do something for me." Bitterness filled his voice.

After a few days he pulled out of the deepest part of the depression. If Joan would go with him to school he could teach. Even though she had changed doctors, she still fought a losing battle with nausea for some months, but she went with him many times to help him teach.

Finding depression an uninvited houseguest, she discovered her rose-colored glasses slipping a little. During the days at home she read and prayed a great deal to keep her own emotions from tumbling into the emotional pit also. During that time she began to pile a heavy burden upon herself. If only she were a better wife, a better housekeeper, a better mother, a better Christian—if only she were a better person, Tim's depressions would not exist.

What did the future hold for them? Fortunately God let her see only the present—and then promised His help in coping with daily problems. Little by little she learned to rely on that strength. At last the depression lifted and Joan's happy, loving husband returned to her.

Chapter 4

Moving On

"It's going to be a boy!" Tim shouted ecstatically. He was just pulling out of a second, milder bout with depression when he had a dream. In it he saw a little blue-eyed blond boy toddling toward him across the floor. From that moment on he told all who would listen that he and Joan were going to have a son.

In May, after the birth of their dark-haired, blue-eyed baby girl, he refused to believe she was really female. Until they got her home from the hospital and he could see for himself, he persisted in believing that someone had made a mistake.

Finally convinced, however, he almost burst with pride. Although Kathi was a colicky little girl who cried a great deal during those first months, her twinkling eyes and sparkling smile totally captivated her father. But even her smiles and giggles could not keep him from plunging again into deep depression the next fall.

Joan dreaded his emotional bouts. Since the school had no phone, she could not call him, nor could he notify her if something came up to detain him. If he was depressed she worried when he was just a few minutes late arriving home. Perhaps now was the time he had chosen not to return at all, as he'd threatened so often. Or had he driven the car into a truck or chosen some other method to end his life?

If he stayed an hour or two later than usual, all Joan could do was worry and pray. A shaking began somewhere deep inside her, making it impossible for her to concentrate on anything.

When Tim finally made an appearance, she had to appear casual. Long ago she had learned that if she seemed upset he would only become angry and more depressed than ever.

"That's just the way I am. If you don't like it, I'll just leave," he had snapped at her once.

To compensate, she put on a calmness she didn't always feel, doing all she could to give both Kathi and Tim a sense of security.

When Kathi was a year old they moved to a town only a few hours' drive from Joan's parents. A short time later a 13-year-old in need of a home found shelter with the Richards family. Joan and Tim both put everything they could into helping Kellie, but her mood swings were the wildest they had ever encountered.

Suspicion of everyone and everything spiked the girl's love-hate relationship. "Who's telling you what to say to me?" she demanded.

"Why, no one." Joan didn't understand what the girl was talking about. "Whatever do you mean?"

"Yes, someone is. He is telling you and my real mother everything to say to me."

Joan recognized real paranoia in the girl's fear of an organized conspiracy against her, but Kellie refused to accept any professional help.

The crisis came one Saturday night as the girl played Monopoly with Tim and Joan. Suddenly she shouted, "You can't make me give up my cat."

Kellie had brought her pet with her when she came. Now no amount of reassurance could convince her the Richards were not trying to get rid of the animal. Screaming all the way up the stairs, she locked herself in her room.

At last Joan and Tim had to call the police.

At first the juvenile authorities thought the problem was just a temporary misunderstanding. Finally the Richardses convinced them that they really did not want the girl to return home unless she would agree to professional help. Kellie refused.

After she had stayed several weeks in the detention center, the judge ordered her sent to a special hospital where qualified psychiatric personnel could evaluate her. Kellie spent some months there before being committed to the State hospital for mentally ill juveniles. Two years later the institution released her to another foster home.

Joan and Tim both had a feeling of success with Kellie, not because they had helped her personally, but because they had succeeded in getting aid for her.

The next school year Joan became deeply involved in the Handicapped Children's School. Handicapped children from all over the State came there to attend. Many of them needed foster homes, not always because there was anything wrong with their own, but just because they lived too far away from the school.

So Denise came to stay. She had a good home and

41

parents who loved her, but because of brain damage at birth, she would never walk without help. Joan thoroughly enjoyed her sweet disposition and the challenge of figuring out ways she could learn to care for herself.

Later in the school year another child joined the family. Having been tied to her bed and locked in her room for the first five years of her life, 6-year-old Tina was an extremely emotionally hurt child. Tim and Joan both worked hard to try to give her the love and acceptance she so desperately needed.

By the time Kathi's little sister Debi brought the number of children in the home to four at the end of that school year, Joan had found a most satisfying "hobby" to fill her time—helping children. Tim too became much involved with them, though nothing stopped his twice-yearly attacks of depression.

One day Tim came home from school extremely upset. "Mr. Jaecks is spying on me!"

"Whatever do you mean?" his wife questioned. "Mr. Jaecks is a professional man, a good principal. Why would he turn to spying?"

"I don't know, but yesterday a private conversation I had with the doctor apparently got back to Mr. Jaecks almost as soon as the conversation ended. I'm afraid to talk to anyone. I know he is watching me."

Joan didn't know what to think. She respected the principal, but now she wasn't sure about anything. Tim was convinced the man had an extensive spy ring who reported to him, and begged her not to trust anyone.

About the same time Tim received an invitation to teach in another State. Thinking of the move took his mind off the problem, and they soon left the area.

Though the transfer meant losing the two foster children, Joan was relieved to discover that they had left his unreasonable fear behind.

Within a few months 9-year-old Kenny and his 6-year-old sister, Renee, joined the family as temporary foster children. It was hard for Joan to understand how anyone could ever give up two such lovely youngsters.

One and a half months later the addition of 2-year-old Allen and his 1-year-old sister, Janet, enlarged the family circle again. At last Tim felt he had the son he'd dreamed of before Kathi's birth. Blue-eyed and dimpled—one blond, the other dark-haired—the two little ones captivated everyone who saw them.

Shortly after his arrival in the Richards family, Allen followed Joan partway down the stairs as she took an armful of clothes under her left arm to the laundry room. As he leaned over the stairway to watch her go around the corner, the boy slipped, plunging headfirst for the concrete floor six feet below.

Joan looked up just in time to catch him with her right arm. She didn't even drop the laundry in the process. As she gently put the screaming little boy down, she thanked God she wasn't half a step faster or slower. Just half a second would have made all the difference in the world.

When Janet was 4, the family received another addition. Recognizing that she was in labor, Joan hurried to the laundromat to get the washing done. Then she drove across town to the doctor's office. Because she seemed so comfortable, he did not believe at first that she was about to give birth.

Finally convinced, however, he instructed her to go immediately to the hospital.

First she had to return across town to pick up Tim. Then they had to drop the younger children off at the sitter before checking in at the hospital.

After Mark's birth three hours later, Tim's joy knew no bounds. Four beautiful daughters and three sons gave him the family he had always dreamed of.

When Mark was just 5 weeks old Joan got a call from the social caseworker. "Would you be willing to take Kenny and Renee's little sister Bev? Her foster family is getting divorced, and we have to move her. Since she already knows you and you have her brother and sister, this might be a good move in reuniting at least part of her family."

"Of course we'll take her," Joan told her after talking it over with her husband.

Shortly after the family's increase to eight children, they moved once again—this time to a beautiful little mountain town where Tim would teach the upper grades in a tiny two-teacher school.

Some of the finer conveniences of life seemed in short supply there. Because of low water pressure, the automatic washing machine wouldn't work. Joan spent many hours with an old wringer machine, placed where the view of the mountains across the valley brought a peace to her soul and a healing to her spirit.

The couple laughed together about the ancient house they had ended up buying. "We should write our own ad for the newspaper," she laughed. "I can see it now:

" 'Five-bedroom house [one room too small for a

bed]: Central heating [an oil stove in the center of the house], daylight basement [half basement dug out under the house]. Secluded mountain setting [no yard, house built halfway up the mountain].'"

Actually the old house bothered no one. All the family thoroughly enjoyed the breathtaking view and the mountain in the back yard. The children spent many hours exploring every inch of it.

One day Joan was bathing two of the children when a shout caught her attention. *"Fire on the mountain!"* Allen and Bev burst into the house.

Tim looked out to discover they were right. The mountain immediately in back of the house was ablaze. He yelled for Joan to get out and he, not wanting to forget anyone, started counting noses.

"Kenny, Renee, Bev, Janet, Allen, Mark——" He broke off. "Where are Kathi and Debi?"

"Right here," Joan said, fastening one more button on Debi's dress. "Let's get out of here!"

Grabbing the dog, they fled by car from the fire that threatened to engulf their home.

"We saw two teen-agers smoking up there a while ago, but we thought they'd left," claimed 6-year-old Bev and 5-year-old Allen.

As the family waited at the school for the firemen to get the blaze under control, Tim questioned the children a little closer about the teen-agers they'd seen earlier. Finally Allen broke down and admitted he and Bev had started the fire themselves by playing with matches. There were no teen-agers.

That night the fire still raged out of control, so the family had to stay with friends.

"What an introduction to a new town," Tim fumed, "burning up seventy acres of mountain!"

"Well," Joan said, smiling, "at least they know we've arrived!"

Fortunately there was no loss of life or personal property, so neither the children nor the family faced any serious repercussions.

During their second year in town, 9-year-old Kathi decided she wanted to earn some money for herself. Since she wasn't old enough to have a paper route in her own name, 14-year-old Kenny signed up for her. Because Kathi was so young, however, the paper route became a family affair. Tim went out most mornings with her, and sometimes the other children joined them to finish the job faster.

Suddenly Tim became afraid to go out mornings.

"I'm scared! You know Mr. Crawford was really upset the other day. I'm afraid he will try to shoot me!"

This time Joan recognized his unreasonable fears as paranoia. Nothing she could say or do would convince him that someone was not trying to kill him.

When the school board decided not to rehire Tim for the next school year, his despair was bottomless. "I'm going to go drive the car over a cliff," he raged. "I'm no good to you, the kids, or anyone else!"

"Tim," his outwardly calm wife answered, "what you do is your decision. You know I don't want you to take your own life. Neither the children nor I would be helped by your committing suicide. Besides, God has a better plan for your life than that."

Gradually he became more tranquil during the night. They prayed together, asking God to take charge of both their lives. With the dawn came peace again.

Often during those years Joan thought of the strange message she felt she'd received from God the night Tim proposed. What did it all mean? If God did tell her to marry him, did that indicate he would eventually be OK?

She really didn't know, but she felt God's guidance in her life and trusted Him to work all things out for her good. While the Lord had not chosen to reveal the future to her, she believed He had given her that experience to strengthen her for the trials He knew would come to her.

As she read the story of Hosea, she discovered that following God's instructions did not always bring instant happiness. The Lord told the prophet to marry a prostitute. He obeyed, and God used his troubles as an object lesson to all Israel.

God's purposes in her loving and marrying Tim were still not clear to her, but Joan knew His promise "I will never leave thee, nor forsake thee" (Heb. 13:5). She trusted Him to reveal His reasons in His own good time—perhaps not even until she reached heaven.

The family made preparations to move again—but where to? By the time another teaching position opened up, Tim was a nervous wreck from worrying over the future. But the job was in a larger school, where Tim would be responsible only for two grades.

About the same time Kenny began to show some serious problems. He had money for which he had no reasonable explanation as to where it had come from. Later Joan and Tim learned that someone had broken into a house near them. Close questioning brought answers that confused things even more.

Much as they loved him, such behavior on a steady basis threatened both the home and the school. Finally they had to let him go.

With the family down to only seven children, the Richardses still found house-shopping somewhat difficult. Shortly after getting settled, Joan found a job to supplement the family income. Since all the children were in school except Mark, her working did not upset things as it would have earlier. Tim took the children to and from school with him, so life fell into a bearable, if rather hectic, routine.

About a year later 12-year-old Renee decided she wanted to leave. Without her big brother, the Richards home just wasn't the same. But the girl threw another problem into the whole situation. She insisted she wanted her little sister with her. Bev did not want to go, nor did Tim and Joan want to lose her.

Then came the long wait and consultations with the caseworker. Would it be better to keep the sisters together? Or should Bev remain in the home where she was well established?

Joan felt sick. The child had come as a 6-year-old. By now, as a 10-year-old, she had become a full-fledged member of the family. How could she bear to lose her?

Taking the problem to God, Joan prayed that He would work all things out. She knew He loved the girl and would allow nothing to come to her that was not best for her. Joan felt she could not just ask God to let her keep Bev, because she couldn't know the future. Only He who did could know what would be best.

But leaving it all in God's hands did little to ease her pain when the authorities decided to keep the two girls together. Bev would have to leave.

"Do you think it would be better for Bev to go to a receiving home during the waiting time?" the case-worker asked.

"No," Joan answered, "it hurts a lot having her here and knowing she soon has to leave, but I know I can help her in a way no one else could."

"In what way?"

"The other day Bev asked me, 'Will my new mamma love me?'

"I knew her first foster mother, so I answered, 'Do you believe Marilyn loved you?'

" 'Yes.'

" 'Do you believe I love you?'

" 'Yes.'

" 'Then you can know your new mamma will love you, too,' I answered."

"That settles it," the woman exclaimed. "She stays with you for the time being."

The day finally arrived when Bev had to go. Through her tears Joan assured her that she would always love her and pray for her—and watched her child walk out of her life.

She would never forget Bev or any of the other children, but now they were in God's hands. Only He could provide for them the love and security they needed.

Chapter 5

Thirst!

"Mom, I'm so thirsty all the time I can hardly stand it!" 12-year-old Kathi said one day.

"You've just gotten back from spending the summer with grandma. Maybe the change in water is bothering you." Her mother didn't feel overly concerned.

"But I was thirsty at grandma's, too. Of course, it was so hot there—that's probably why I was thirsty all summer."

Busy with her job and taking care of the five children, Joan quickly let a little thing like a child's thirst get pushed out of her mind.

"Kathi, would you do the dishes tonight?" she called next evening.

No answer.

"Kathi? Where are you?"

Finally she found her oldest daughter in bed. "What are you doing in bed at six-thirty in the evening, honey? Are you sick?"

"I don't think so. I'm just so tired. May I please go to bed now, Mom?"

"Of course, but first let me take your temp." Joan

51

was sure the girl must be sick. No 12-year-old ever went to bed during the day voluntarily—did she? But her temperature was normal. "Here's a glass of water, honey. You get some sleep. I'll do the dishes tonight."

A few minutes later Kathi entered the kitchen. "I need another drink."

"I thought you'd be asleep by now," Joan remarked. "You seemed so tired."

"I think I did doze off a little, but then I had to go to the bathroom. Now I'm thirsty again."

Kathi had always been a quiet child, but now even books failed to hold her interest. She would doze off on the first page. But tired as she was, she could not get a good night's rest. She would get to sleep only to wake up every hour or so to go to the bathroom and get another drink.

And her weight plummeted. Though her appetite was insatiable, she was so thin her mother could see her ribs sticking out. Joan began to be concerned. She knew that one of the symptoms of diabetes is excessive thirst—and several members of her family had diabetes. She decided to make an appointment for the girl to see the pediatrician.

Meanwhile, she decided to take Kathi to work with her rather than send her to school. Her daughter could not sit through a class without having to leave the room, and Joan just wanted her where she could keep an eye on her.

Kathi was not able to make the forty-five-minute trip to the office without stopping to go to the bathroom and get a drink. At work the girl helped with some packaging and other routine jobs. When she'd get too tired, Joan let her put her head on the desk and doze off a few minutes.

"Can we go out to eat?" Kathi asked.

"That sounds like fun to me," Joan replied.

"I want a milkshake for dessert."

"OK, honey. Let's. You know if the doctor says you have diabetes you won't be able to have sweets anymore."

"Will I be sick all the time?"

"No, my cousin has diabetes and he's a doctor," Joan explained. "You may have to take insulin, or maybe pills, or maybe we'll be able to control it with diet. I don't know exactly."

"What's insulin?"

"It's something your body is supposed to make to help take care of the sugars in your system, but if you're diabetic your body isn't producing enough of it. You might have to give yourself shots every day to get the right amount."

"Oh, I hate shots!" her daughter exclaimed.

"I know. I don't blame you. We'll just have to wait and see. You'd better enjoy that milkshake, though, because it may be the last one you get!"

The next day Joan took the girl to her doctor's appointment.

"Is something wrong?" the physician asked.

"No, not really. It's just that I'm awfully thirsty all the time," Kathi explained.

"Since we have so much diabetes in our family," Joan put in, "perhaps she should be tested for that."

"I rather doubt it at her age." He didn't appear too impressed with the possibility. "Who in your family has diabetes?"

"Well," Joan began, "I have a cousin and an uncle, besides my mother and aunt, who are borderline cases. Oh, and my sister. I almost forgot her."

"You're not diabetic yourself?"

"No."

"Did any of your relatives become diabetics as children?"

"No, I believe they were all adults."

"Well, we're probably looking at a kidney infection or something else quite simple."

Although definitely not an alarmist, the doctor did ask the lab to give him the results of the testing right away, probably just to put the mother's concerns to rest. While they waited, he stepped out to see another patient. After a few minutes he returned and chatted happily with Joan and her daughter.

When the lab findings came back, Joan saw a shocked look cross his face before he turned to the girl. "Kathi, how under the sun did you ever manage to have such a brilliant mother? She was right! You do have diabetes! We'll get you into the hospital and fixed up in no time, though."

"Can it be controlled by diet, or will she have to take insulin?" Joan questioned.

"All diabetic kids have to take insulin," he explained. "For most things, catching the problem at a young age is better, but with diabetes, the younger the patient, the more serious it is. Kathi's lucky she's as old as she is—but she will have to learn to give herself shots."

Joan took her daughter to Children's Hospital and watched as they attached IVs and gave her her first shot of insulin. Since her mother and the doctor had explained so much to her, the girl was not terribly frightened. Knowing her mother was not afraid, because she understood a little about diabetes, helped tremendously.

In fact, Kathi had no desire to go to bed at all. She hadn't been that sick to begin with, and with the first insulin she received, her system rallied quickly, giving her back her normal energy. She kept getting up and running around, dragging her IV stand behind her. Finally the nurses in the intensive care unit told the doctor that Kathi didn't seem to need much intensive care. He could move her to the ward.

Joan dropped by the hospital administrator's office to tell him her daughter was in the hospital. He was a personal friend of the family, so she thought it might help the girl if he could find the time to visit her.

"What happened? Did she go into a coma?" the man asked immediately.

"No, I recognized the symptoms and took her to the doctor's office to be checked."

"Wow, that's really unusual," he exclaimed. "Most of the time when a kid comes in with diabetes, it's first discovered because the parents can't wake him up. You're really fortunate you figured it out before then."

In the hospital a parade of nurses and dieticians brought instructions regarding the special diet Kathi would have to follow, along with techniques for giving herself shots, and the other special health-care details needed by a diabetic.

She would require a carefully regulated, balanced diet for the rest of her life. If the amount of insulin was too much to take care of what she ate, she could pass out from low blood sugar. On the other hand, if the amount of insulin was not enough, she would gradually build up too much sugar in the blood—and that would put her in a coma.

The doctors explained that she must follow a strict routine so she could take her insulin and have her meals at a definite time every day. That would help in getting her system settled down so she could live as normal a life as possible. Even with careful monitoring, it would probably take about two years for her system to stabilize.

"At first the pancreas will sometimes kick in some insulin too, so your blood sugar can vary quite a bit," the doctor said. "Later the pancreas will give up and let us regulate things. It's a lot easier then."

A little frightened over the huge responsibility of regulating an unpredictable pancreas, Joan took Kathi home at last. At first they checked with the doctor daily about the insulin dosage. Later Kathi would be able to determine the proper amount for herself by testing her own urine.

About a week after Kathi came home from the hospital Tim began his usual fall depression. Worried about Kathi, and remembering the doctor's warning about maintaining a calm routine, Joan did all she could to keep his problem from the children.

As her life became more and more hectic, and the financial pressures became more acute, Joan became deeply concerned over her oldest daughter. If Tim didn't get back on his feet soon, total support for the family would rest on her shoulders—and that included Kathi's major medical expenses.

The girl would not be able to wait until the next paycheck to get her insulin, as she could a new blouse. The strict diet she needed was more than Joan could afford—yet Kathi had to have the proper foods *every* day. They could not even allow her shoes to wear out too much, since any small irritation could cause an infection that would be difficult to heal.

Joan didn't know all the details of the family's financial picture, but she knew her salary was a necessary *supplement* to Tim's. If her income were all there was, she was afraid the family faced total ruin—and she might even lose her daughter in the process.

The whole world seemed to be caving in at once. Her life was shattering into little bits around her. Kathi's diabetes, Tim's illness, financial pressures—just plain daily survival seemed too much to hope for.

Then Mary Edwards' offer *by Monday* to help with the children gave her the thrill of seeing God work in her life.

More assistance came when her sister Laurie offered to take Kathi. After talking it over, they decided it was probably the only intelligent decision to make. Kathi would have the proper diet and medical care, her routine would be calm, and Joan would be able to concentrate on other problems.

But she missed her daughter intensely. Part of her was glad Kathi was not under the pressures they had at home. Yet another part wanted her *home*. Joan needed the help she had learned to rely on from her oldest daughter, and Kathi was homesick. She needed her mother too.

Debi suffered from the separation even more than her mother and sister did. The day they took Kathi to her aunt's, Debi cried as though there had been a death in the family. Joan wasn't sure she could cope with the experience as the girl continued crying wildly all the way home. Finally Joan gave her a tranquilizer, to calm her.

Debi continued to be lost and heartbroken for weeks. Perhaps she only used the separation from her sister to express the heartbreak she felt over her father's illness and the general insecurity that life was handing her.

But God brought good even out of this. Gradually, as the weeks and months passed, Debi and her mother drew closer together. The new emotional bonds helped both of them as they prayed and talked together about many things. The year that started so hard brought a new independence to Debi as she became her own person instead of just her big sister's shadow.

Chapter 6

Bankruptcy!

Meanwhile, though Joan had made strides in handling some of the problems at home, Tim was not making equal progress toward mental health. Instead of his stabilizing on the medication, emotional changes occurred even more rapidly than before. In five minutes Tim could shift from deep depression to overactive giddiness. Then he might lapse into paranoid fear. To further complicate his emotional roller coaster, his hands shook violently all the time, because of the medication he took.

Usually he weighed about 170 pounds. Now he determined he would break 200. With a deliberate attempt to gain 30 pounds in a month, he ate everything in sight.

After Tim had been in the psychiatric ward several weeks, the school board that had employed him asked Dr. Willerton to check on his condition. Joan wondered how her husband would be during this visit. Which personality might he show? He understood some things about his own condition, but he was not too perceptive about what caused his changing moods or what he could do to control them.

When told that Dr. Willerton planned to visit, however, he managed to shave and get dressed to leave the ward for the interview.

Tim appeared fairly stable for the short time he talked with the superintendent. Of course, Dr. Willerton could see some changes, such as the extreme weight gain and the shaking hands, in spite of Tim's best attempts to cover them. Therefore Dr. Willerton recommended to the school board that they hire a permanent replacement so they could salvage the school year in the best way possible.

Out of a job, Tim plunged into frantic desperation. No medication could calm his despair. No therapy could soothe his fear. He used the phone in the ward to call all over the world, looking for work. Of course, he charged all those calls to his home phone.

Already deeply concerned over their financial situation, Joan knew that she simply could not pay the mounting phone bill. She contacted the phone company to ask what she could do.

"I'm afraid there's nothing much you can do," the company representative told her. "As long as you're married to him he can charge anything he wants to your phone, and you will be responsible for paying for it."

"What if I get an unlisted number?"

"Well, that would work only so long as your husband did not learn the new number. Of course, there's an extra charge for switching to an unlisted number."

At last Joan decided that she would simply have to take the phone out. At least that was one bill that would not continue to grow.

The other bills had become so huge in her mind that she could not bear to open them when they arrived. With no money to pay them, no promises to make to her creditors, she felt like following the example of the proverbial ostrich and burying her head.

Once again her sister Laurie came to the rescue. "Just send all your bills to me, along with whatever you can afford to put on them. I'll make contact with your creditors and tell them the situation."

With a tremendous relief Joan mailed them to her sister—unopened. The problem was finding any money to send along with them.

But when Laurie discovered that they totaled more than ten thousand dollars, it completely dismayed her. "Joan, I don't see any possibility of your ever taking care of all of these!" she exclaimed. "I don't see any way out for you except bankruptcy."

Because she worked for an attorney, Laurie decided to type up the proper form Joan needed to file for bankruptcy. Then she sent the completed list to Joan with the advice "The sooner you file, the better off you'll be."

"You're probably right," Joan sighed, "but somehow I can't do it yet."

Then she talked over the situation with her employer, and showed him the full listing of debts.

"There must be some way out besides bankruptcy," he mused. "You know it is against company policy to keep anyone on the payroll who has to go bankrupt."

"But that would mean we would have *no* income!"

"Yes, I know." He tried to be kind. "I don't make the policies, and we don't want to lose you. But I won't have any choice if you have to declare bankruptcy. By the way, have you checked on filing alternative? You know that is a way of giving you time to pay your bills. You put on them only what you can each month, and the court gives each creditor his share. That is one possibility for avoiding bankruptcy."

"I've understood that allowance for tithe-paying is not included if I file alternative," she responded. "With my financial situation, this is no time to neglect God!"

"No, I understand. It does seem clear, however, that you will have to do *something*. Keep us informed on what you decide."

Frustrated, Joan went back to her office. Bankruptcy or alternative? She figured for a few minutes and concluded that she would have no money to put on the bills each month if she did file alternative.

Bankrupt! The very word held terror. Even the family's furniture would go—and no job for her afterward, either. Of course, she knew that her secretarial skills would make it easier to find another position, but would she have the courage in the present circumstances to face job hunting? And if she got one, could she think clearly enough under the emotional pressures to learn new routines? She didn't think so.

Closing her office door, she put her head on her desk and cried quietly for a while. The whole world seemed to be crashing around her at once.

"Lord," she cried, "what do You want? I only want Your will. If it is Your will for me to be bankrupt and jobless, I'm willing. I'm willing to work for You wherever You want me, but I'm also willing *not* to work at all. If you want me to become *nothing* and live on welfare for You, I'll do it."

Gradually peace came to her as she made the strangest surrender of her life. She had always thought it meant being willing to go wherever God wanted her to, to be willing to do whatever He desired her to do. It had never occurred to her that surrender might also include being willing to be a *failure*, to be *nothing* for Him, to even be willing to live on welfare for Him.

Then, she remembered the text in 1 Corinthians 10:13: "There hath no temptation taken you but such as is common to man: but God is faithful, who will not suffer you to be tempted above that ye are able; but will with the temptation also make a way to escape, that ye may be able to bear it."

That passage had entered her mind several times lately, but she pushed it away, thinking, That doesn't apply. I'm not being tempted to do wrong.

Suddenly it dawned on her that temptation did not always involve a matter of doing wrong. Hard times could also pressure one to let go of God, to refuse to trust Him anymore. It would be easy to wonder whether God Himself could solve the problems she now faced. Reduced to its simplest elements, she realized, that question is what the great controversy between Christ and Satan is all about. Can we trust God or not? Satan claims we can't. It is up to us to decide—and the decision to trust Him or not is what determines one's salvation.

She looked up the text in her Bible. In growing excitement she wrote down the verse, substituting the word *trial* for *temptation*. "There hath no *trial* taken you but such as is common to man: but God is faithful, who will not suffer you to be *tried* above that ye are able; but will with the *trial* also make a way to escape, that ye may be able to bear it."

Of course! God would provide a way of escape from even her present circumstances if she continued to put her confidence in Him.

The phone rang. "This is Mr. Snell from the car leasing company. We're getting a little concerned over your payments. We'll need two payments by the first in order to keep your account in good standing."

"I don't know what to do," Joan cried. "My husband is in the hospital and unable to work. I'll need more time to decide what I must do."

"Well, I'm sorry. Our time is running out. Of course, you can turn the car back in. Then you will owe only eight hundred dollars as the fee for not completing your lease agreement."

"Eight hundred dollars! It might as well be a million!"

"You might consider bankruptcy," the impersonal voice on the other end went on. "Naturally, we can work with you that way. But we do need to hear from you by the first."

The doctor's remark about a man in Tim's condition buying "a house, a yacht, and a car all in one day—with fifty dollars in his pocket" came to Joan's mind. That's the way our finances are—but we don't seem to have the house, the yacht, or the car to show for it, she thought.

She looked down at the text she had written a few moments before. Lord, You've promised, she reminded Him silently. Where is my way of escape from this trial?

With her courage bolstered by God's promise, she went back to work. All those advertising brochures still needed to go out tomorrow, bankruptcy or not. When she left her office to work in the mail room for a while, on impulse she took with her the promise she'd written earlier.

When called again to the phone a few minutes later, she read the passage again before answering. "Lord," she breathed, "You've promised to allow no trial more than I can bear. It says so right here. Please be with me."

Another creditor awaited her on the line. But when she explained the situation, she received kindly understanding.

"Of course we'll give you the time you need. Just keep in touch so we know what your plans are."

"Thank You, Lord," she whispered as she hung up.

She found that having a promise written on a card so she could carry it with her helped tremendously. Just knowing it from memory was not sufficient. She required something more tangible, something she could touch and see. The heavier the pressure, the more she must *know* God's promises were real.

Now another problem began to worry her. Janet and Allen were still foster children with the family. Although Joan and Tim had applied to adopt them, nothing was final as yet. She realized she had to go to the caseworker and explain the whole situation. After having the children since infancy, Joan knew she couldn't stand the thought of losing them, but she had to inform her of the latest developments.

Making arrangements with her supervisor to take a day off, Joan determined to be at the Social

Services office as soon as it opened.

"I need to see Mrs. Smythe."

"I'm sorry. She's out of the office for the day. Would you like to speak with her supervisor?"

"Yes, please." Joan feared that if she put it off, she would never again have the courage to face the problem.

"I really don't want to get involved," the woman remarked. "It would be better if you can wait and talk with Mrs. Smythe. I am willing to listen if you need to talk with someone now, though."

"I'm afraid I do want to explain the situation today," Joan replied. "My husband is in the hospital right now with a serious nervous breakdown. The doctors really can give no assurance that he will be OK or even able to return home."

"I'm so sorry. What do you want to do?"

"I don't know. I do know I love Allen and Janet and don't want to lose them. If they had been born to me, you wouldn't decide I was an unfit mother and take them from me just because of my husband's condition, would you?" Joan felt as if she were pleading for her very life.

"Of course not," the supervisor agreed.

"I've had these two children since they were babies. They don't even remember any other mother. Wouldn't it be better for them to have one parent than to lose both at once?"

"Yes, I see your point." The woman's sympathy and understanding made the interview much easier. "Of course, the decision is not up to me. I'll tell Mrs. Smythe you were in and ask her to get in touch as soon as possible."

Another wait. It seemed to Joan that was all she

ever did—wait for other people to decide whether her life should be a shambles or not. Suspense was good for her figure, however, since she could barely eat when under pressure. But eating something three times a day helped to keep her emotions on a better level, so she learned to choke some food down. Sometimes it might be only half a glass of milk or a piece of fruit, but it helped.

"Lord," she prayed, "give me strength. Give me wisdom to know Your will, and then the courage to do what You tell me."

Again as she prayed and read, a Biblical passage came to her. Isaiah 49:25 states, "For I will contend with him that contendeth with thee, and I will save thy children."

"Lord, whatever happens, I know You love Allen and Janet even more than I do. Please save my children as You promised. Work things out so they will be OK."

The next morning Joan had barely walked into her office when the phone rang. Mrs. Smythe's voice came over the line. "I didn't want you to worry one more minute about the children. I have no intentions whatever of taking them from you."

Just from the release of tension she started to cry. Praise God! He still controls the universe after all!

The caseworker went on to explain that no matter what decision Joan had to make, the department was there to help. Even if Tim could not return home, Joan could adopt the children as a single parent.

In the midst of all the pressures, Joan felt her heart going out in praise to God for His goodness to her. She could understand Isaiah 43:2: "When thou passest through the waters, I will be with thee; and through the rivers, they shall not overflow thee."

True, the waters of trouble in her life were flooding around her, but with God by her side they would not overflow her. *God would never allow any trial too great for the two of them to be able to carry together.*

Chapter 7

Unfit!

According to the list of debts Laurie had typed up, Joan owed well over ten thousand dollars. It did not include such items as the telephone bill, which had climbed to almost unbelievable heights before she had the instrument taken out.

The school board had decided to let Tim go, but now another committee would meet to determine the details of the termination settlement. As the time for the meeting approached, Joan again felt unbearable pressure. So much rested on its decision. She took her problem to the One who owns the universe. "Father," she pleaded, "please sit on that committee for me. I want You to be in charge of my situation, not the people on it."

The day of the conference came. While she waited for it to conclude, Joan saw a friend she had known from childhood. She knew he was on the committee, but since he lived out of town, she had not expected him to be present that day. It relieved her to know that God had brought him there for this particular meeting.

Finally the group reached a decision. Tim had

not actually taught since the first of October. They could have considered it as his date of termination. The committee, however, decided to consider the whole month of October as sick leave. The termination settlement began as of November 1. That extra month gave Joan a total of two thousand dollars.

After this money was gone Joan would have nothing but her own salary to support a family of seven—and take care of all debts. Obviously, if she didn't declare bankruptcy, her creditors would soon force her to do so involuntarily. But still she hesitated to make such a drastic decision.

A few days later the hospital released Tim. "I'll be coming home to stay," he declared happily. "The best medicine will be just to be with my family. You know what I need is to be home, where I can go to bed until I'm well."

That frightened Joan. She knew that the worst possible thing he could do would be to stay day after day in bed with nothing to do. It wasn't like a broken leg, when one must remain off it to allow it to heal. For the mind to heal, the body should stay busy.

"If Tim does return home and follow through with his plan of going to bed," the doctor explained, "I'm afraid he will deteriorate very rapidly. Bed rest does help with some types of physical problems, but the mind is different. Tim's work for a while should have no pressure, but the only chance he has of ever stabilizing is if he gets a job and keeps himself busy."

"What can I do?" she wondered out loud.

"I'm afraid that, with his mind set on going to bed, all you can do for him is tell him he can't come home right away. Hopefully, the need to support himself will push him into working. He absolutely must stay active. Besides, I really don't feel it's safe to have him home with the children at this time."

Joan now found herself forced to make the most terrible decision of her life. She wanted Tim with her. Surely she could help him somehow. Then she thought back over the past thirteen years and realized she had done all she knew to aid him from the earliest days of their marriage. All she had accomplished was that he had broken anyway to the point where he no longer could work at what he was trained to do.

Would it be possible now, when Tim was so much worse, for her to succeed where she had failed before? And what about the children? Could she really work, take care of five children and keep them safe, *and* nurse her husband?

It certainly would do no good for anyone if she pushed herself to the breaking point. Besides, Tim might work to support himself and be able to return home. Though separation definitely was not her choice, Joan at last had to decide, with a breaking heart, to tell him he could not live at home at that time.

Even he understood when she explained her reasons. He wanted to come home strongly enough that he was willing to try to cooperate with his doctors for his own recovery. Since he needed to remain near the hospital, where he could continue as an outpatient, they decided he would stay with friends for a while.

He began working as a dishwasher in a nursing home. After a day and a half, however, he walked off the job. Deciding to visit his father, he borrowed money from the people he was living with and left by bus.

His father, determined to do all he could to help, made an appointment for Tim to see a local Christian psychiatrist, and planned for him to remain with him for a time.

Meanwhile financial pressures forced Joan to file for legal separation. It would take some pressure off the family's finances and would also enable her to be in legal control of the children's safety.

With her heart breaking, she made the decision to cut off a part of her life. As she did so, she had no way of knowing whether Tim could ever take his rightful place again in her life. Much as she loved him, she knew she could not take care of him and still manage with the children.

With Kathi gone, Allen at 9 shared the position of the oldest child with Debi, who was just two months younger. Then came 8-year-old Janet and finally 4-year-old Mark.

Joan felt most concerned about Janet. Hyperactive, with deep frustrations, she was quite a difficult child to handle. Her dark, naturally curly hair, olive complexion, and loving disposition made her an especially attractive and lovable little girl—but that temper! Even before his breakdown, Joan and Tim had asked the caseworker for a psychological evaluation of Janet so they could know how to help her better.

When the day of the appointment arrived, Joan took the girl to the Social Services office where the psychologist would test her. While Janet was with the psychologist, Joan talked with the caseworker for a while. They assured her that the examination of the girl would take only an hour.

When the psychologist finished, he sent the child to a playroom so he could talk privately with Joan and Mrs. Smythe. "I find Janet quite immature," he began. "Do you know of any reason why this should be?"

"No, not really," Joan admitted.

"Well, I'm afraid you're subconsciously holding her in babyhood," he continued. "In fact, by the time she is 13, she will be a monster no one can live with."

Joan couldn't believe her ears. "What can I do to help her more?" she asked through the tears that already began to flow.

"Nothing. The only hope for her is to get her into a good foster home immediately. You shouldn't waste any time if you want to minimize the damage already done to her."

By now Joan sobbed openly. "What can I do to help her even during the time I will have her?" She was still deeply concerned over the child and wanted to help her, no matter how much it hurt.

"The only thing you can do is get her out of your home. I'm sure if I could examine the other children in your home, I'd see the same pattern of immaturity in all of them. If you ever decide you'd like Janet back, I think you would have to receive extensive counseling before you would be ready." He nodded to the caseworker and left.

"Well, it looks as though you'll have to get Janet ready to leave," she said sadly. "I had so hoped you'd be able to keep her."

"I can't get her ready," Joan sobbed.

"You'll have to. You did it for Bev. You must do it for Janet now," she said firmly.

73

"I can't. She wouldn't understand." Joan left in tears.

That evening she told the children she was sick and Debi would fix their supper. Lying on the couch with her face hidden, she cried quietly. Not wanting the children to know anything about her upset, she tried to hide it all from them under the pretense that she was ill. As a matter of fact, she didn't have to fake it at all—she *was* ill.

Where was God now? Did He still rule her universe, or was someone else in charge of her life today? Joan didn't know. She couldn't think, or even pray, coherently.

When Debi tried to give her something to eat, Joan's stomach rebelled. Only the dog understood her feelings. He tried to lick the tears away, whining softly all the time. Though she had succeeded in keeping the problem from the children, she couldn't fool Precious. She smiled through her tears at the little animal's concern.

At last she just asked God to hold her as He would a small child. Picturing herself comforted by her heavenly Father, Joan fell asleep at last.

The next day was Sabbath, usually Joan's happiest time of the week. Today everything seemed draped in black. She had nothing of herself to give to the children. In fact, she couldn't even take them to church, much less attend herself, for she would have to face other people and pretend to be in one piece.

After a while she thought over Janet's problems and what the psychologist had said. When the girl was 7, she had had a severe convulsion. The parents had rushed her to the hospital, which had run tests to determine the cause. The verdict had been an irregular brain-wave pattern that the physicians said could cause many problems. From that time on the doctor had her on medication to control seizures.

However, the drugs seemed to make her harder to handle than ever. She had been an explosion of activity from the minute she joined the family. Now her temper became an even bigger problem. Gradually, however, over the next year Janet had calmed slightly, and Joan felt the girl was making some progress toward self-control.

Is it really my fault that she has a problem? Joan wondered. I certainly didn't cause her convulsion, nor the irregular brain-wave pattern. Why, the psychologist didn't even know she was on medication to control seizures!

Several other things he had said bothered her too. He had claimed that if he could examine the other children, he was sure he would find that they demonstrated the same pattern of immaturity.

That's just not true, she thought. The other children show none of the problems Janet does. Besides, how can he tell on one evaluation whether she is getting better or worse? I know she is calmer and easier to live with now than she was a year ago. How can he be sure she will be a monster by the age of 13?

By Monday morning Joan no longer felt depressed. She was mad—fighting mad. Never before had she realized how really *good* anger could feel. As soon as she got to her office she phoned the caseworker.

"I want a psychiatric evaluation of both Janet and me," she requested. "If I caused all of her problems,

I'm certainly in need of a great deal of help—but there is no way I caused her convulsions or irregular brain-wave pattern. I'm not consciously or subconsciously holding her in babyhood. Therefore I want a second opinion!"

"Well," the woman responded coolly, "I think perhaps we can go along with you on that. After all, you do have a lot of years invested in both Janet and Allen. I'll give you the name of a good psychiatrist the department uses quite a bit. I know he believes in taking a child from his home only as a last resort. We'll see what he has to say after an evaluation."

"Thank You, God," Joan breathed. She didn't have a definite Yes, but she had gained a reprieve from the sentence passed on Friday.

A friend attempted to help. "You shouldn't try to take on the added responsibility of two more children under your present circumstances," she said. "You should be thankful you have only the three children to worry about without trying to add on two more."

"I'm not *adding* any more," Joan sputtered. "And I wouldn't want to take on more either. But I've had these two now for seven years."

"No one would ever blame you if you did give them up, you know," the friend persisted.

"I couldn't. They might not be mine legally, but they're still mine in every other way. I love them too much to ever give them up."

The children had been so little when they first came that they had wrapped themselves securely around both Joan's and Tim's heartstrings. They had looked on the Richardses as their parents for so long now that Joan felt that all concerned would only suffer needless hurt if the authorities came and took them from her.

Whatever happened, Joan could only rest on the promises of God. Without Him she knew she would not survive. Only her core of faith held her together. The testing knife could not cut through that core—but it could hurt!

Chapter 8

God's Storehouse

Two thousand dollars to cover ten thousand dollars in bills, Joan mused to herself. Obviously impossible!

She knew her salary could not stretch to make payments on all those debts after taking care of living expenses. Either she must take what she needed from Tim's termination settlement to pay the bankruptcy filing fee, or use that money to pay a few choice bills.

As usual she prayed about it. Second Kings 4:1-7 records the story of the widow whose sons the creditor planned to sell to pay her husband's debts. The prophet Elisha told her to borrow jars from her neighbors and then pour from her own meager supply of olive oil into them. She obeyed and the oil continued until she had filled all of the containers she had in the house. Then she sold the oil to pay the debts.

"Lord," Joan pleaded, "please help me to know what to do. I don't believe that you want me to go bankrupt. You showed the widow in the Bible what to do. Please help me."

The holiday season was drawing near when one of the other secretaries in the company where Joan worked asked, "What are you doing for Christmas?"

"I'm afraid that with Tim sick we really can't afford Christmas at all this year," Joan replied.

"Won't you even have a tree?" she persisted.

"I really don't have the money. I just don't see how we can manage anything."

The other girl expressed her sympathy, and both went back to work.

A few days later Joan was eating in the lunchroom when one of the women employees called for quiet. "We think it's time for Christmas to come to the Richards family," she announced. Someone else set a huge box in front of Joan.

She couldn't hold the tears back.

"See, I told you that's what she'd do," someone said, half laughingly.

"I believe every person here has contributed to your Christmas, Joan," the president of the company added. "We wanted you and the children to have a merry Christmas in spite of your husband's illness."

Unable even to thank them properly, Joan could only cry. "Lord, thank You," she breathed.

Later she wondered whether disability insurance covered any of the family debts. Joan knew that life insurance covered some types of loans, but what about disability? She decided to check.

To her joy she learned it did take care of a loan and one car (not the leased one). If Tim was ill, all she needed was an insurance form signed by the doctor, and the insurance would automatically make the payment.

When she subtracted the two bills from the

$10,000 total, the new figure was only $4,000. Two thousand dollars was 50 percent of that. The odds were improving.

Joan knew that if she had to declare bankruptcy her creditors would get nothing. Might they accept a settlement of 50 percent?

She mentioned the possibility to her attorney. "Well, it can't hurt to try," he remarked.

Remembering the creditor who had been so understanding earlier, Joan decided to call her first. If that company turned her down she knew she would not have the courage to contact another.

"Mrs. Lindstrom? This is Joan Richards."

"Oh, yes, I remember. How is your husband?"

"Not too well. I'm afraid he's not responding to treatment. Mrs. Lindstrom, on my salary alone I can't make payments to all my creditors. However, I do have a termination settlement that is enough to pay 50 percent on my bills. My only alternative is bankruptcy—and then no one would get anything. Would Fashion House consider a 50 percent settlement?"

"I will have to take this to the general manager," the woman responded, "but I know he will agree. I believe all your other creditors will, too. I'll check and get back to you with a definite answer in a day or two."

As Joan hung up she breathed a prayer of thanks, pleading at the same time for God to touch the manager's heart so he would be receptive to a settlement. Unable to muster the courage to contact anyone else until the store made a decision, she waited in an agony of suspense for two days before Mrs. Lindstrom called her back.

"They'll do it!" she cried.

Joan personally took a check for one half the amount owed to Fashion House, which accepted it as payment in full.

Now armed with a little stronger faith, she decided to ask her attorney to contact the car-leasing company. When he phoned, however, the response was not quite what they had hoped for.

"Settle for $400? No way! We'll see Ms. Richards in bankruptcy court before we'll make a settlement of any kind. The amount she'll owe if she breaks the lease agreement by turning the car in early is $1,200. We won't accept nothin' less!"

Their figure had grown from $800 to $1,200. But Joan decided that she would go ahead and approach the other creditors, leaving that one until last. If the company forced her into bankruptcy, at least the others would get something.

"Don't you ever wonder, *Why me?*" a friend questioned.

The question came as a shock. "Yes," she admitted slowly, "but it seems to be turned around. Instead of 'Why do You allow these terrible things to happen to me?' I keep wondering, 'Why are You choosing me to do so much for?'" Evidences of God's love and care constantly balanced the terrible pressure Joan always felt.

When she contacted a loan company, they refused a half settlement—but agreed to cancel all interest on the loan. The figure was almost the same.

Joan soon learned that any file clerk has the authority to *refuse* a settlement. Only top management can *accept* one. She asked for the top every time she made a contact.

Her request angered one credit manager. "If you decide to make a settlement like that, don't think you can ever get credit from Mace's Tire Shop again! We'll accept a settlement if we have to, but we won't ever do credit business again with you."

The last thing Joan worried about at the moment was credit. She didn't care if she never saw a credit card again in her life. What she was concerned with was survival.

Finally, after much prayer, Joan personally contacted the leasing company again.

"How do I know yer husband ain't fakin' sick?" the man asked suspiciously.

"I can get you a signed statement from the doctor if you'd like."

"No, never mind. We'll settle for five hundred dollars," he growled. "But we won't give you no signed statement sayin' we'll do it before we get the money!"

Dismayed, she didn't trust the man and feared he might bill her for another seven hundred dollars. Finally Joan sent the money to a friend who lived in that city. She took it in personally to the company and received the statement "Paid in Full" in exchange for five hundred dollars cash.

A few days before Christmas a friend came by the house. "Let's go get a Christmas tree!" the man announced.

The children were excited. "Goody! A Christmas tree!"

The whole family piled into "Uncle Charlie's" car to help pick just the right tree. He had acquired the honorary title of uncle because he had been the children's friend since they were little.

Joan smiled at their enthusiasm. Because of the lump in her throat, however, she had a hard time expressing her appreciation for his kindness. I seem to cry just as much when someone does something kind as I do when everything is going wrong, she thought wryly.

Christmas Day arrived. With Tim still with his father thousands of miles away, Joan tried by herself to make the holiday special for the family. They had the gifts from the office under the tree, and the excited children wondered what they had received. When they opened the presents and discovered some much-needed clothes, plus a small toy for each of them, their merry Christmas seemed assured.

Suddenly the sound of the doorbell interrupted their noise. Tim stood outside.

"I'm home to stay. I'm fine, and everything's great!" he announced.

But Joan had just heard a few days before from his father that things were not good at all. In fact, he was extremely concerned about his son's condition.

She watched him with the children for a while and saw changes take place before her eyes. A short time after arriving home he was sitting in his chair, immobile with depression.

Remembering the doctor's warnings about possible danger from him unless he really did stabilize, Joan feared to let him stay. She loved her husband and hoped and prayed he would be able to return home someday—but was now the time?

Joan felt that with Tim home she had a time bomb in her living room—and she didn't know when it would explode. Slipping from the room, she talked the matter over with her best Friend. "Lord," she prayed, "what should I do?"

Again prayer gave her the assurance she needed. She knew she had tried to help her husband with depression for thirteen years—only to have him collapse anyway. Now, in his illness, he had slipped to a place she could no longer reach.

Since the children were still young, she could still reach them—and she was all they had. The idea of raising them alone frightened her, but 2 Corinthians 12:9 promised that God's grace would be sufficient for her.

Tim would have to leave.

When she told him as gently as she could that he could not stay, he was hurt, but at the same time he understood why she had to make such a choice. In his calmer moments he assured her many times that he felt she had made the right decision. Of course, he still intended to return as soon as possible.

It was hard on the children to have their father home and then watch him leave again. Their Christmas turned to tears as he walked away.

Tim decided to get an apartment downtown and try to get a job as a taxi driver. A company hired him immediately, but he worked only one day before deciding to return to the hospital. He asked a friend to take him to the nearby State mental hospital and checked himself in. Two days later he signed himself back out and returned to driving a cab.

By now all the creditors but one had accepted the 50 percent settlement Joan offered. Though one gasoline company had accepted, another gave a flat No.

The official notice disturbed her: "If this account is not paid in full by January 15, we will institute proceedings to garnishee your wages."

She called the credit office. "My husband has had a nervous breakdown and is unable to work. I don't have this kind of money. Is there any way you can accept a 50 percent settlement?" Each time Joan made the request, she felt as if she were pleading for her life.

"I'm afraid our company won't do that kind of thing," the cold voice on the phone said.

"Could I speak with the credit manager or the general manager? I need to speak to someone authorized to make a settlement."

"I'm sorry. I am the credit manager—and we won't make any kind of settlement."

"There is simply no way I can pay this by January 15." Joan felt the situation was hopeless. After she had come so far with so many creditors, one company was going to force her into bankruptcy.

"If it will help, we can give you a little more time. You can pay one third January 15, one third February 15, and the last third March 15. I'm sure if you explain the situation to your employer he will give you an advance or figure out some way to help you. But we need those payment on the dates I've mentioned if you are to avoid legal action."

"OK. Somehow I'll try to make the payments." Although she didn't know *how*, she had no choice but to try. One thing she was sure of was that she didn't want to ask her employer for such a large advance. She would never succeed in working one of that size back down.

Since she had enough left over from the termination settlement to make the first one-third payment, she sent it off.

A little-known Bible story that she ran across by accident bolstered her faith again. Second Kings 3 tells the story of the Israelites in battle with the Moabites. Unfortunately the Israelites had no water for themselves or their animals. Elisha instructed them to dig ditches, "Ye shall not see wind, neither shall ye see rain; yet that valley shall be filled with water, that ye may drink, both ye, and your cattle, and your beasts."

The next day, when the Israelites awoke, enough water filled the trenches for all their needs. When the enemy saw the morning sun shining on the water, they thought it was blood. Deciding that the Israelites must have quarreled among themselves, the Moabites rushed down to finish them off. Because of the Moabites' lack of organization, the Israelites won a great victory that day.

"Lord," Joan prayed, "I don't know *how* You can provide the money I need to make these payments, but I believe You can. The Israelites didn't know how You could provide water for them either, yet You did. Please help me."

Then Tim decided he could help. Still driving a taxi and making enough to support himself, he agreed to give Joan all he could toward the gasoline bill.

Not knowing how long Tim might be able to work, she could only rest on God's promises. All the money in the world belonged to Him, and He could give it whenever He wanted to. With Tim's help she made the second payment on time.

"Thank You, Lord," she whispered. "Just one more to go."

March 1, two whole weeks early, she completed

the final installment. Joan could hardly believe Tim was still working after two months.

At three o'clock on the morning of March 4 the doorbell awakened her. Rushing to the living room, she was startled to discover her husband climbing through the front window.

"You've got to take me to the hospital right away," he shouted. "I can't stand it! Hurry!"

In his panic he was almost incoherent. Joan woke 9-year-old Debi to tell her what she was going to do. She didn't know whether she would be back in time to take the children to school, and someone needed to know where she was going. Then she quickly dressed for the trip to the hospital.

As she drove, she managed to piece together some of the reason for his fear. While he was on duty that night, lights began to come at him. In a desperate attempt to avoid a collision with one of them, he had almost wrecked the taxi. Another driver had brought him to the house.

Tim had been able to work just long enough to pay off the one company that wouldn't settle for 50 percent. In fact, God had held him together for four extra days.

Later Joan discussed with her attorney how she had succeeded in avoiding bankruptcy. "What have you got that no one else has?" he asked in astonishment. "I've known a lot of people who have tried to get a settlement like that through, but I've never known of one who succeeded."

"If he had told her that before she made the attempt, she might not have had the courage to try. But Joan knew what it was that gave her success where others had failed. She had God.

Her favorite author wrote, "Our heavenly Father has a thousand ways to provide for us of which we know nothing."—*The Ministry of Healing,* p. 481. Joan hadn't known of any way in which God could help her avoid bankruptcy—but He knew a thousand.

Chapter 9

Janet

During all the time of financial crisis the problem of Janet hung like a dark cloud over everything. The caseworker, concerned over the family situation, insisted that Joan must come in each Friday afternoon for a conference.

Since it was her only free afternoon, it added a great deal of stress to an already full schedule. Friday afternoons represented the only time she had for shopping, cleaning house, paying bills, doctor's appointments, and all the other million-and-one things she had to do. When Tim was in the hospital in her sister Laurie's hometown, she left on Fridays to visit him. Later she still made the trip frequently to see Kathi.

The emotional stress of those Friday afternoons put far more pressure on Joan than just the lack of time. Each week Joan dreaded those friendly little chats with Mrs. Smythe. Not that the caseworker wasn't a nice person—she was. But Joan knew that Janet's whole fate, and perhaps that of Allen as well, rested on the woman's decisions.

While the caseworker supported Joan in many

ways, Mrs. Smythe was almost all-powerful. Joan knew that the judge would probably accept the woman's recommendations without question. Mrs. Smythe had indicated to Joan earlier that she might allow her to adopt the children as a single parent if Tim couldn't return home, but Joan hadn't made any final decisions. All she could do was wait to see how Tim would be—and Mrs. Smythe was willing to give her whatever time she needed.

At last the day came when she would see the child psychiatrist about Janet. Dr. Rossi, a short, fat little man, was quite pleasant to talk to. He decided that before the next appointment she should do a little homework. "I want you to write Janet's history as completely as you can, giving me everything you know from birth on."

Although Joan didn't have much information about Janet's birth, she did know that the authorities had placed the child in foster care when she was only 2 weeks old. As far as Joan could tell, the girl's development had been normal through infancy.

When she came to the Richards family two days before her first birthday, Janet exploded into hyperactivity. Then the first Sabbath when Joan took the children to church, a girl exclaimed, "Why, isn't that Allen and Janet?"

"Yes, where did you know them?"

"Their foster family attends the church where I baby-sit on Sundays. I've taken care of these two for months."

"Tell me all about them."

"The mother would bring them both in and put Janet in the crib. She'd say, 'Just leave her alone.

She'll be fine.' Then she would put Allen on the floor to play with the toys, and leave. Allen would play quietly the whole time—but Janet was something else. She would lie in the crib and bounce in a kind of rhythm until her mother would come get her."

Janet's hyperactivity was so pronounced Joan began to wonder whether she had been kept in a playpen. That might account for her extreme curiosity about everything around her. She decided to ask her friend from the church to check for her. "Yes, I'll be glad to," she agreed. "I'm sure I can find out for you."

A week later she reported triumphantly, "I checked with an acquaintance of their foster family. They had Janet in a playpen all the time, and Allen too was kept closely confined."

"What do you mean by 'confined'?" Joan asked.

"They said he was allowed to play in one room only."

That explained it! Janet had never known the joy of investigating the world, nor had she learned the meaning of the word *No*. After all, no one would put a no-no in a playpen just to teach a baby what the word means.

By the time Janet was 2, she was talking as fast as she was running—but it wasn't English. When someone couldn't understand her she refused to repeat herself. She would just put her head down and cry from frustration.

Finally Joan became convinced that the girl was making sense to herself, if to no one else. She decided to make a special effort to understand her. To her amazement she actually heard Janet talking backward. Words, phrases, even whole sentences tumbled out in reverse.

Although Joan had never heard of such a thing, she started teaching Janet to speak English. The child's determination equaled her problem, and gradually her speech became comprehensible.

Joan had to watch the girl especially closely. Because of her hyperactivity, she could get into things faster than her foster mother could get her out of them.

One day Joan cleaned out the dresser drawers in the girls' room. Suddenly she realized that she could not hear the child anywhere. Checking quickly, Joan found her in the kitchen. Janet was safe and sound—but the kitchen wasn't. Cheerios, Wheaties, oatmeal, and flour dumped in the middle of the kitchen floor made the nicest "sandpile" to play in.

Joan started sweeping up the mess, only to discover that the child was missing again. Hurrying down the hall, she found her back in the bedroom— with all the newly cleaned dresser drawers emptied out onto the bedroom floor.

When Janet disappeared another time, Tim and Joan drove through the neighborhood after sending the children searching in all directions. All the activity attracted the attention of several neighbors, who joined in to help hunt for the little girl. A man living about a block away noticed them and came over to ask, "Are you looking for something?"

"Yes, our little girl," Joan exclaimed. "She's just 2, and she disappeared about an hour ago."

"She's safe and sound at our house," he assured her. "I found her down by the highway, starting out into the cars. I knew she didn't belong there, so I brought her home. We just called the police to report having found a child."

"We were just going to call them too," Joan said. "Thank God that she's OK.!"

Janet's frustrations always showed up quickly. Her problems with talking and her hyperactivity gave her reasons to get extremely upset quite often. And when disturbed, she made sure everyone knew it. She could scream for two hours at a time.

No discipline or love seemed able to stop the terrible spells. When Joan talked to her doctor about the speech problem, hyperactivity, and terrible temper, he just shrugged. "She hears well, so she's probably just tuning you out. It seems to me that you have a discipline problem."

But nothing worked. The one thing Janet had in her favor was a strong determination. When Joan could enlist that will on the right side, nothing could stop the child. Then, too, no matter what Janet did, no one could keep from loving her. Even perfect strangers noticed her sweet smile and outgoing personality. More than once, people wishing they could have Janet approached Joan. If they only knew!

Once a neighbor chatted at the front door for a few mintues. Mrs. Thompsen knew as well as Joan did to stay alert to Janet. How that little 3-year-old slipped past them both they never did figure out, but suddenly they realized she was missing.

When they couldn't locate her in the house, Mrs. Thompsen ran home to check on the possibility the girl might have gone there. There she was, happily eating cigarettes and the neighbor's medicine. Wet pills and half-chewed cigarettes littered the house.

Because they didn't know how much of either she

had actually eaten, Janet had to have her stomach pumped out. But that wasn't the only time. The same treatment followed when she ate toadstools from the yard.

When Janet was 7, another problem showed up. The Richards family had gone to a program in the city, when the girl began to run a fever with no warning. She fell asleep on Joan's lap.

Suddenly a loud groan broke the quietness of the auditorium. The child's arms and legs began to work in the pattern Joan recognized instantly as a grand mal convulsion. Joan carried her into the women's restroom, followed immediately by two nurses and a doctor. He confirmed the diagnosis she already knew and urged her to take the girl immediately to the Children's Hospital.

By the time the parents got her into the car, Janet was quiet again. At the hospital, for the first time the doctors were ready to listen as Joan described the child's problems. Testing revealed an irregular brain-wave pattern that the doctor said could cause all kinds of problems. He prescribed a medication to control seizures, and at last allowed Janet to go home. "This should not only prevent any further seizures but also help calm her behavior," the pediatrician assured them.

Janet had no more epileptic seizures, but the hyperactivity and emotional upsets increased dramatically along with a sluggishness in moving and responding. The doctor only shrugged when Joan told him what she had observed. "In time this should help," he commented.

Joan continued to give the girl the medication four times a day, afraid to stop for fear she might have another convulsion. The doctor wanted her to stay on it until she was 12 to 14 years old.

Now 8, Janet's movements were slowed by the heavy drug dosage, but her activity level still remained high—and she had no emotional control.

Carefully Dr. Rossi read the history Joan wrote, and then indicated he would like to meet the whole family, including Tim, who was out of the hospital and driving a taxi at the time. They set up a date in February for all of them to come in, with the exception of Kathi, who was still at Laurie's.

As he observed the children, Dr. Rossi quickly concluded that the pattern of immaturity the psychologist had seen in Janet was *not* evident in any of the others. The girls' problems were uniquely her own.

Dr. Rossi explained that with her kind of history, along with the evidence of the irregular brain-wave pattern, they should not be surprised that Janet might be immature. "But so what?" he questioned. "Many people are immature all their lives, yet they get along quite well. You are doing all you can to help her, and doing a good job of it at that. What more can anyone expect?"

"Then you don't think her problems were all caused by my trying to hold her in babyhood?" Joan questioned.

"Certainly not," he chuckled. "I don't know what was the matter with that psychologist. I can't imagine any professional coming to the conclusions he did. If Janet were moved, it would probably destroy any chance she has of becoming a mature person. You're doing a good job with her. All that I could possibly ever ask of you is that you hang in there with her until the job is done."

At the same time, the separation between Tim and Joan concerned Dr. Rossi, who asked the two of them to return.

"But we can't afford to pay you," Joan protested.

"Since the caseworker set this up for Janet's benefit, I'll work it out so the State pays me," he growled.

In subsequent visits Tim covered his problems fairly well (as he always did with any doctor or when in the hospital), and Dr. Rossi became convinced the separation was unnecessary. At his urging, the couple decided to try marriage once again. Tim moved home.

With Tim working and back in the family, everything seemed so much better to Mrs. Smythe that she told Joan she didn't need to continue coming in every Friday. But at home Joan could see his moods swinging rapidly from depression to excitement to fear to anger. She never knew what to expect from one minute to the next. The strain of living with his emotional shifts was hard on everyone. By now the children understood so much more that they felt the pressures too. Joan could no longer insulate them from Tim.

Then came the 3:00 A.M. panic and the trip to take him back to the hospital. It was a relief to Joan and the children to know he was safe and being taken care of properly.

As Dr. Rossi continued working with Janet, he discovered other problems only hinted at so far. Janet not only heard things backward (sometimes called auditory dyslexia), she also saw backward (visual dyslexia).

Joan had recognized that counting was hard for Janet. The girl couldn't find a page number, understand the idea of one less than, or work easily with the alphabet. The lack of natural sequencing ability caused other handicaps, such as a difficulty in distinguishing between more and less.

Concept such as over and under, in front of and behind, and many others tended to reverse themselves. No wonder Janet frequently felt frustrated. She really couldn't understand the world around her, nor could she easily express her own needs and desires. Yet she was intelligent.

A direct question always sealed her lips. When she was little, "What is your name?" brought only "I don't know." However, Joan discovered she could tease her into answering.

"I'll bet your name is Suzy," she'd say.

"It is not. It's Janet," she would answer triumphantly.

Obviously she knew many things if someone could only give her the key to communication. Dr. Rossi explained that Joan would probably need to give extra support to the school for many years if Janet were to learn to communicate effectively.

Since she had already had the experience of teaching Janet to talk word by word, Joan understood a little of what he meant. Janet could learn in a short time on a one-to-one basis with her what her teachers despaired of ever getting across to her.

Now with Tim back in the hospital again, it seemed to Joan that her heartache began all over again. How could she go on alone?

Though some might offer sympathy because she had the responsibility of the children, Joan knew they were not really a liability—they were her incentive to keep on trying. Without them she might never have seen the necessity of winning through prayer.

With a heart full to overflowing with thanksgiving and pain at the same time, Joan turned her attention again to the smaller problems of daily routine.

Chapter 10

The Bitter
and the Sweet

Now Joan had to make another decision. When the hospital released Tim, should he return home? Or should they separate again? She was not only concerned about the children's safety and emotional health, she was worried about herself.

Because of the heavy strain she had endured for almost six months, she could no longer sleep without taking tranquilizers. Although she never took anything during the day, it was a relief to be able to turn everything off at night.

Then she ran across an article about tranquilizers that brought out the fact that people's reasons for taking tranquilizers were identical with those for drinking. Furthermore, the article went on, the effects on a person's judgment, self-control, and personality were the same.

Joan knew she would never use alcohol to relax because of pressures, but was she doing the same thing to herself with tranquilizers? She decided that she didn't need them anymore.

Again a text came to her attention. "I shall both lay me down in peace and sleep" (Ps. 4:8). I guess I'll have to trust God to get me to sleep, too, she decided. It's just one more area in which I'll have to put total confidence in Him.

After being in the hospital for a month, Tim decided to check himself out. In their State anyone who signed himself into a mental institution could also let himself out at will.

Joan talked with the doctor. "Is he ready to be released?"

"No, definitely not. In fact, I don't believe he's in any shape to be home."

Unfortunately Tim refused to accept the physician's conclusion. "If you won't take me home," he threatened his wife darkly, "I won't be alive by morning."

"Tim," she said sadly, "I can't make your decisions for you. I know suicide is not God's choice for you. He has such wonderful plans for you if you'll only trust Him to take charge."

"You'd better check on me in the morning. I don't expect to be alive. I mean it."

"That decision is between you and God, Tim, not between you and me." Joan knew she could no longer hold herself responsible for his choices. She could only support him as much as possible and stand by to help.

The next morning she did stop by his apartment. She found him sitting on his bed, too groggy to finish dressing himself. "I'm s'prised I'm alive," he mumbled.

"What have you taken?" Joan asked.

"All m' pills. I d'know. I can't get dressed."

Joan helped him get his clothes on. Then came the job of trying to steer him down three flights of stairs. As overmedicated as he was, he walked like a drunk. They finally made it to the car.

This time the hospital would not let him just sign himself in. They asked the court for an involuntary commitment. The judge's office decreed that if he wanted out against his doctor's advice again, the hospital could hold him for twenty-four hours to seek a further court commitment.

About the same time Joan finally made up her mind to change from legal separation to divorce. It was not a happy decision, but at least it was a decision. Anything was better than another six months of uncertainty. Besides, she could (and would) remarry him if he stabilized.

One day Tim's doctor called her long-distance at her office. "I have some questions I need answered. Tim said you'd be the best person he knew of to help me."

"Surely, what can I do?"

"I've been wondering about a lot of things," he began, "and I'd like to know more about what your church teaches."

"I'll be happy to answer anything I can," Joan responded, surprised to find Tim's doctor at the State mental hospital interested in the topic.

"How does the church feel about psychiatry?" he wanted to know.

"So far as I know, nothing but respect. There are many Christian psychiatrists in our church."

"Are there any in this town?"

"No," Joan answered, "though I know of several in the city."

"That's too bad. Tim wants to stay here in town when he is released, and I feel it is important that he have a Christian psychiatrist to follow up."

Now Joan *was* surprised. She knew that some doctors regarded religion as a hang-up. They concentrated their efforts on getting people over such "problems." But Tim's doctor felt he should have a Christian psychiatrist.

"What does the church teach about medical personnel working on Saturday? What is the basis for Saturday observance anyhow? Why is church membership necessary? What about baptism?

Joan answered each question as fully as she could. When he hung up an hour later, she breathed a prayer that God would guide the man in his search for Him.

A month later the doctor felt Tim was ready to try living again outside the hospital. He made arrangements for him to receive welfare payments, since Tim feared to drive a taxi anymore.

The next Sabbath at church Tim and Joan were both totally surprised to find the doctor there. Joan immediately notified the pastor.

"Yes, I am aware that he's here. Tim gave him my number too for help with his questions, and he got in touch with me last night. Do you know he was raised in the church?"

"No, I had no idea."

"Well, he was, and he's planning to return after forty years away from God," the pastor informed her happily.

"Thank You, God," Joan prayed, "for showing me at least one good thing You've been able to produce out of this whole experience. I'll continue to trust You to bring good to each of us."

Tim decided to use his first month's welfare

check to pay his bus fare across the country to visit his mother. He would return the first of June.

Another phone call at the office upset Joan. "You can't just kick a man when he's down by filing for divorce like you're doing," a friend protested.

"I'm not trying to kick him when he's down." Joan pleaded for understanding. "I'll do anything I possibly can to help him."

"Look, you married him 'for better or for worse.' Now, I'm sorry things turned out 'for worse,' but you're married and you should stay that way."

There were people in Joan's office, and by now she was crying, so she excused herself and went into her boss's office to continue the call in private. Half an hour later, when her employer started into his office, he took one look and backed out.

Finally the friend gave up, even though Joan had not been able to convince him she had acted on the doctor's advice. She would be happy to remarry Tim if he could stabilize, but in the meantime she knew that pushing herself to the breaking point would be no favor to Tim, the children, or herself—and she knew she was about as close as she ever wanted to get to that line.

Another bill arrived in the mail. For some reason Joan never understood, a health spa Tim had joined a year before had just now got around to wanting their money. She went in to talk with them personally.

"I don't have any money, since my husband has had a nervous breakdown. Besides, I don't feel this is really my bill. This is for *his* membership, not mine."

"We don't really care whose membership is

involved," she was told. "Since you were married to him at the time he incurred it, you are liable. If you don't pay it within a reasonable time we will have to garnishee your wages."

Unable to do anything more about it at the moment, Joan put it, too, in God's hands.

Early in June, Joan received a phone call from Bert, a friend of many years. He needed a mover's assistant and had heard of her husband's collapse. Hoping to help, he asked Tim to ride with him. Since Tim enjoyed nothing more than traveling, it was an easy decision.

Shortly after starting to work with the truck, Tim arrived back in town for a weekend. Joan hadn't seen him so relaxed and clear in his thinking in a year. The whole weekend was almost as though they had stepped back in time to their courtship days.

As they walked together in the park while the children played, they began to make tentative plans for a future together. They hesitated to set definite dates, but if he could maintain what Joan could see that weekend, she knew she would remarry him before too many months went by.

One evening about a week later Tim began to hyperventilate so much that Bert had to take him to the emergency room of the nearest hospital, where an injection calmed his breathing. When it happened twice more during the next two weeks, he began to have second thoughts about his assistant.

As they approached Joan's office on a return trip with the truck, Bert said casually, "I think you should go back into the hospital, Tim. If you're planning to go to school in another month, you need to get squared away again."

"But I'm fine," Tim protested. "I'm not depressed or anything—and I love trucking."

"But I can't take the risk of needing help for you sometime in the middle of the night when we're miles from nowhere. I really do believe you should check into the hospital again for a while so they can get you in top shape for school. I'll drop you off at Joan's office so she can take you to the hospital, or back to your apartment if that's what you want."

Tim felt completely puzzled. He thought he was really doing great, and now this. "I guess I don't even know anymore when I'm OK and when I'm not," he told Joan.

She could see the hurt and bewilderment in his eyes as she drove him to his apartment. He didn't feel he needed to go back to the hospital right then.

Getting his old job back as a taxi driver, he attempted to settle down to a routine again. But the lights still tried to collide with him, and he became terribly afraid someone would kill him in the cab, so a couple of days later he quit.

Joan tried to talk him into going on welfare again so he could concentrate on attending school. Since he could no longer teach, the State would pay for his retraining under their disability program.

But Tim determined to work full time and go to school, as well. He got a job working nights as an orderly in a nursing home. Mornings he attended school, reserving afternoons for sleep. Most evenings he went to the house to spend a little time with Joan and the children.

Although the judge had decreed that Tim had no visitation rights, Joan never denied him access to his family. She knew that if she saw signs of danger, she had the legal right to ask him to leave—and call the police if necessary. But if he had had regular visitation privileges, he could have maintained his rights no matter what shape he was in. Joan felt much safer knowing she *could* ask him to leave, but she didn't ever want to have to do it.

Meanwhile Joan and the children barely scraped by financially. After having the phone taken out she still had to pay that huge bill. She made arrangements with the utility company to pay ten dollars on the bill each month.

Then there was that health spa. They still threatened to garnishee her wages if she refused to pay them, but she didn't have any money.

Once again she went to them to plead her case. "This is *Tim's* membership. I really don't feel totally responsible for it."

"Well, you were married to him when he signed the contract, so we will collect from you," the clerk said.

"Look, Tim has been able to work this summer and has some money laid aside. I believe if you will send him a bill he will pay it."

"We don't care which of you pays it, but you're the one we're billing."

"But I don't have the money—and Tim does," Joan cried in desperation.

"Lady, all we want is our money. You've got a good job and he doesn't. If you don't pay, we'll have to garnishee your wages."

"All you'll accomplish is to push me into bankruptcy."

"Well, if things are that bad, probably you should go bankrupt."

"Would you *please* just try billing Tim directly?" she tried again.

"OK—but when he doesn't pay, we'll see you in court."

With no question whatsoever, her husband paid the bill as soon as he received it, which took one more worry from her mind.

She sewed a great deal, making most of the children's clothes. Cooking was cheaper if done from scratch, so she bought no quick foods or mixes. Even the smallest purchases she carefully thought over.

The one big problem was shoes. She couldn't make them, the children couldn't just go without, and the budget couldn't afford any.

The children's caseworker checked to see whether there was any kind of aid available to the family, but Joan made too much at her job. Social Security might pay something someday, but there was no point in putting through an application until a person had been unable to work for a year. Of course, Tim had been employed at various times since his break, so he probably couldn't qualify for any kind of disability anyway.

"The silver is mine, and the gold is mine," God declared in Haggai 2:8. She could only trust Him to continue to supply all their needs as He had been doing for the past months.

Chapter 11

A Tent or a Cottage?

"OFFICIAL NOTICE TO VACATE PREMISES. This is to notify you that you must vacate these premises within thirty days."

The notice she found on the door one evening when she got home from work stunned her. *Vacate the premises in thirty days!* She opened the small white note attached to the official document.

"We're sorry to have to ask you to move—you've been a good tenant—but we've sold the house, and the new owners want to move in."

Joan sank into a chair, unable to think what she should do. Move! But where to? Houses for rent were not plentiful, and she certainly had no money to buy one.

She had looked for reasonably priced rentals before school began, since she knew Kathi would be home again. On her budget Joan realized she could never afford to keep her in the dorm. Besides, the other children would find life much easier if they lived close enough to the school to walk.

But time for school rolled around with no house in sight. Kathi started the term in the dorm, and the other children still had to commute. Mary Edwards had finished out the previous school year, taking them to school, as she had promised. But now the children attended a different school. Joan took them each morning to another friend who kept them (again without charge) until time to catch the school bus.

A month after the beginning of school Kathi caught a cold that progressed rapidly to an upset stomach. Worried because of her diabetes, she called her mother at work.

Immediately Joan told her boss and left the office. When she got Kathi home she began to realize she had a rather sick girl on her hands. By that night Kathi was vomiting, and Joan decided she would feel better with her daughter in the hospital. Joan knew that stomach upsets are serious for a diabetic, since it is difficult to balance diet against the right amount of insulin.

One o'clock in the morning found them on the way to the nearest hospital. Because Kathi had just returned home from Laurie's, she had no regular local doctor. All they could do was hope someone qualified to handle diabetes might be available.

In the emergency room of the hospital Kathi spent the time waiting. With the extreme thirst understood only by diabetics, she thought she would die when the nurses refused to give her anything to drink. They were afraid her nausea might cause her to vomit. However, the girl couldn't stand not having anything. Finally Joan gave her small sips to relieve the dryness of her mouth.

After two hours of waiting the doctor on duty told them the blood tests indicated a high blood sugar level, and advised Joan to take the girl to Children's Hospital an hour away in the city.

By 4:30 A.M. Kathi was finally admitted, and Joan was free to return home. Exhausted Joan took ninety minutes to make the forty-five minute trip home. She arrived just in time to get the children off for another school day.

Then she left for work as usual. She had deadlines to meet and she shouldn't miss the day.

During her lunch hour she visited Kathi at the hospital and was grateful to see her daughter responding to treatment so quickly. Within a few days the girl returned home.

But Joan now hesitated to let her go back to the dorm. So she added the half-hour trip to and from the academy to her daily routine.

Now she had arrived home and found the notice to vacate. "Lord," she prayed, "what now?" She didn't even know where to begin.

When she recovered a little from the shock, she drove to the academy and contacted a realtor in the area. The agent knew of no rentals, but did suggest that perhaps Joan could qualify for a low-income government loan to buy a house.

That sounded good to her, so she went to the Farm Home Administration to see whether she could meet their requirements. Wonder of wonders, she did! They told her how to go about things and gave her a list of some homes in the area within her budget.

Joan began house shopping in earnest. She found one ideally situated, but the owners couldn't decide whether to rent or sell. In fact, they were so indecisive she couldn't even discuss business with them effectively. Besides, she was not convinced the house would pass a fire inspection. The chimney ran up between the two upstairs bedrooms. To get out of the second one, a person had to go through a narrow hallway past the chimney. Remembering her own home burning when she was 5, Joan felt nervous about the situation.

The next house she looked at didn't look like too much on the outside, but inside the owners had remodeled it, and made it spacious and comfortable. Joan loved it. But FHA said the price was too high.

Then the realtor sent her to the Neuman house. Situated in the country on a half acre, it was really a cute little place. She fell in love with it at first sight. Since the bedrooms were small, however, she planned to make two more in the existing garage.

When Joan decided to talk personally with Mr. Neuman, she found a man desperate to get out from under heavy financial pressures. With his wife leaving him, he knew he would lose the house along with his good credit rating if he couldn't sell soon.

"I'm already two payments behind. And I'd be willing to give the house to you on a take-over-the-payments deal just to get out from under this load."

"I'd be glad to work out a deal like that. In fact, since the payments are lower than the rent I'm paying now, I'd be able to make those two payments you're behind—over a period of a few months, of course." Joan knew she couldn't handle the extra expense all at once, but felt she could pay it a little at a time.

"Well, I think we've reached a verbal agreement," Mr. Neuman said, extending his hand. "Let's shake on it, and I'll go down in the morning to get the papers drawn up for us."

Joan felt a tremendous release of tension as she drove home that night. A home at last!

Impatiently she waited all the next day for the call from Mr. Neuman telling her the papers were ready for her signature. None came. The day after, she tried to phone him, but the man did not answer. That evening she drove by the house. No one was home.

Finally a week after her verbal agreement with Mr. Neuman, Joan received a call from her realtor. "I think you have a right to know what has happened. The head of our agency liked the deal you worked out with Mr. Neuman. In fact, he decided he could offer him a better one, so he has bought the house."

Joan was incredulous. "The head of the agency has actually bought the house out from under me?"

"Yes, he did. I didn't like it, but I felt at least you had a right to know. Of course, it is still on the market—for ten-thousand more than it was—if you're still interested."

"I don't think so," she choked. Then she began to cry from the total frustration of having the solution yanked away from her just as she reached for it.

Later a friend reminded her, "God never allows a door to shut unless He will open a better one."

"I know He won't let me down," Joan said, wiping the tears away, "but it still hurts."

Back to the beginning again. Now Joan had only about two weeks left before the deadline. "Lord, I need Your help *now*," she pleaded.

Having noticed a house near the academy with a "For Sale by Owner" sign in the window, she decided she had nothing to lose by checking, so she called the number listed.

"Might you be willing to rent the house?" she asked.

"No, we really prefer to sell," the woman answered.

Joan searched constantly. Nothing was available large enough for a family of six and still within her financial limits. In fact, she found nothing of *any* size that matched her pocketbook.

Joan decided to claim Hosea 11:11: "And I will place them in their houses, saith the Lord." She certainly needed one! If "man's extremity is God's opportunity" *(The Acts of the Apostles,* p. 146), she was certainly giving God an excellent one.

Finally, in desperation she telephoned to ask again about the home "For Sale by Owner."

"My husband is showing the house this evening," the woman said. "But if the people don't take it we would be willing to lease to you. The house is my mother's and she is just getting too old to live alone. We don't want to leave the place vacant, so we'd be willing to rent to you if they don't buy it."

"Lord, if this is Your house for me, You work it out," Joan prayed. "I don't know how to do anything more. It's in Your hands now."

If God works on flaws in character, Joan thought, I certainly must have a weakness in the area of patience. All I do is wait.

The next day the call came. "We've decided to lease the house to you."

"I was praying you would." Again Joan thrilled at the evidence of God's hand in her life.

She went over to see the house and sign the lease. Though it had only three bedrooms, she found they were large enough that the family would have room for comfort. Situated on three and one-half acres, it offered the convenience of closeness to the academy, along with the privacy Joan loved.

"If you'd like to save installation charges on the phone, we can just add your name to the listing. Later we'll take the other name off. It'll save you quite a bit on getting a phone in."

Joan truly appreciated their thoughtfulness. Although she had the old utility bill paid off by now, she could not have afforded a phone if she had had to pay installation charges.

In order to help her, the landlord was even willing to forego the usual first and last months' rent. The cleaning and breakage deposit required was minimal.

With her copy of the signed lease in her hand, Joan took time to thank her heavenly Father. Without Him she would not have made it.

Tim agreed to help her move the Sunday before the deadline, so she made arrangements to take a few days off from work. She would have Thursday and Friday to pack, and Monday and Tuesday to clean the old place after the move on Sunday.

Joan almost felt she was moving onto holy ground. God had prepared one of His own houses for her.

Then she thought of the cramped little place she would have been in if God hadn't said No. Although Joan gave the realtor no credit for good intentions, she had to admit that God worked even through his greed to arrange things for the best. The house He gave her was closer to the school, larger, more private, and just plain nicer than the one the realtor had bought out from under her.

"If God be for us, who can be against us?" Joan

understood Romans 8:31 a little better now. Even Satan's attempts to hurt her through the realtor's action fell to nothing. With God on her side, no one could harm her.

Chapter 12

Through the Valley

Tuesday dawned cold and beautiful. Fall leaves had turned their brilliant hues and rustled in the breeze. The mountains in the distance already had begun to show off their white caps against the clear blue sky. As Joan drove to the office that morning, her heart went out in gratitude to the Creator of all things.

Tim still worked at the nursing home nights and attended school in the mornings. Joan thought she could see some progress toward stability, which kept alight a small spark of hope. Perhaps he really would make it back home someday.

That day Joan tried to get twice a normal day's volume of work done. After all, she had only Tuesday and Wednesday before taking four days off to pack and move.

In her efforts to finish up, she did something she almost never did. She stayed about fifteen minutes after quitting time. Not that she was afraid to put in extra time. In fact, she sometimes worked through her lunch hour to get things done, but she didn't work after five o'clock. Since a friend kept the children without pay each day after school, Joan felt she dared not take advantage of the woman's willingness to help by being late.

Tonight Joan picked the children up from the sitter's before swinging by the academy to get Kathi. After a short stop at the store they were finally ready to go home.

As they turned the corner of their cul-de-sac, 5-year-old Mark shouted, "There's an ambulance!"

Joan quickly took in the scene. "Yes, you're right. I wonder what it's doing here?"

At the bottom of the little hill, right in front of the Richards home, stood a police car. Little groups of neighbors gathered outside their homes, watching curiously.

Mark noticed Tim's car parked in the driveway. "Goody! Daddy's home! There's his car!"

As Joan brought her vehicle to a stop, the children piled out, and Mark went racing for the house to see his father. A policeman approached her and asked courteously, "Are you Mrs. Richards?"

"Yes, I am."

"Could I talk with you privately for a few moments?"

"Of course." Joan had the sinking feeling it concerned her husband.

"I'm afraid I have bad news," the officer went on. "Your husband apparently committed suicide today."

"Suicide!" Joan thought perhaps it was only another attempt, not the real thing. "Is he really dead?"

"Yes, he's dead. He has apparently been dead for some hours."

All she could think to say was "Thank God he didn't do just half a job." She was not glad Tim was dead, but she felt a strange relief that he was not some kind of living vegetable doomed to breathe on for years with no mind.

"Will you be all right?" the officer questioned.

"Yes, I think so," Joan said slowly. "He had a nervous breakdown a year ago and hasn't been able to be home since then. I guess we've already been through the worst of things."

"So often this kind of thing leaves the family with so many problems," the policeman commented kindly.

"Who found him?" Joan wanted to know.

"Some neighbor children. It seems your husband had taken a sleeping bag and pillow and made himself comfortable outdoors near the car exhaust. He just fixed up a way to direct the fumes toward himself and went to sleep."

Joan thanked the officer for his kindness. She would have expected him to be either coolly professional or stammering for words in an uncomfortable situation. He had not gone to either extreme. Instead he had offered compassion and understanding.

Now she had to break the news to the children. "What happened, Mother? Where's Daddy? What did the policeman want?" they all asked at once.

"Let's go inside, kids, and I'll tell you." Joan wanted to get away, from the eyes of the curious neighbors, where she could explain things in privacy.

Though she knew it would hurt, she intended to tell the children what had actually happened. She felt that the truth coming from her in love would pain them far less than the taunts of some classmate if the children didn't already know.

"I'm so sorry, kids, but daddy took his own life today," Joan began. "He just made himself comfortable with a sleeping bag and pillow, breathing the exhaust from the car until it killed him."

"Why did he come *here* to do it?"

"What did *we* do to make him want to hurt us?"

"Why did he use *my* sleeping bag? And *my* pillow?" Kathi wailed. "What did *I* ever do to hurt him?"

"I think I loved daddy the most of anybody," Mark sobbed.

"Why did daddy break his promise?" Janet cried. "He promised he would bring me a surprise Wednesday night. He broke his promise, 'cause now he won't come Wednesday!"

Why, why, why?

But their mother didn't know why. She tried to put her arms around all five at once. If only she could kiss away their hurt as she had always soothed away skinned knees and bumps. But she couldn't just kiss it away.

She felt as though she were drowning in a sea of anger—and she hadn't expected that particular emotion. No one had told her that sorrow and anger are very close to each other. She was prepared to comfort the children's sorrow, but she really didn't know how to handle their rage.

"I don't want to stay here," one of the children wailed.

"OK," Joan agreed. "Let's get out of here. Where do you want to go?"

"To Mary Edwards' house." The children still felt

close to the woman who had helped them through the past school year.

They arrived at the Edwards home just as the family started to sit down to supper. Mary immediately reacted in her usual practical way to a crisis. "You folks sit right down and eat. Now I really insist." She refused to take No for an answer.

Joan and the children ate the Edwardses' supper that evening. They never learned what—if anything—their friends ate that night.

A little later Joan used their phone to make the necessary calls to notify family and friends.

The news stunned her boss. "I didn't think Tim would ever do that. I'm so sorry. I know your kids need you. We won't expect to see you until next week."

"Since I'm in the middle of an evangelistic campaign," Tim's father said, "it's a little rough, but I'll come. If you can arrange to have the service on Thursday evening, I'll have to miss only one meeting. I can get another pastor to take it the one night."

"I'll do my best," Joan promised.

"Thanks. I'll have to fly back that same night to make it in time for the next meeting."

Tim's mother and sister felt they could not get away, but his brother planned to attend. Joan's pastor agreed to conduct the service whenever she could schedule it.

At last Joan finished contacting those who needed to know. She gathered the children together to take them back home.

"Do we have to sleep in our own rooms tonight? Please, Mom, can we all sleep in the living room?"

Sensing that the real problem was that the

123

children felt too insecure to sleep alone, Joan gave her permission. The entire family shared the same room. Joan wanted to do all she could to show the children that she was still there and loved them.

The next day Joan went to the funeral home to make the necessary arrangements. "I have no money. What can I do?" she inquired.

"If my sister were the one in your situation," the funeral director began, "I would tell her what I'm telling you. Welfare will pay all expenses for the funeral if you apply. The only thing is that you must file the application and get it approved *before* the service."

Knowing that Tim would never want her to spend money she didn't have after he was dead, Joan went ahead with arrangements for the Social Services agency to pick up the tab for the funeral.

"Did your husband leave a note?" the funeral director asked.

"I don't know," Joan admitted. "If he did, the police must have taken it."

"Well, I think if I were you I'd call them. They can at least read it to you if they have one."

She decided to follow his advice. Using the phone at the funeral home, she called several departments before finally getting the right person on the line.

"Yes, Tim Richards did leave a note," the voice affirmed. "Just a moment and I'll get it from the file." Joan waited while the man located the letter. "Here it is. It's written on blue paper. It looks like some kind of personal stationery with the name 'Tim and Joan Richards' printed at the top."

"Yes, I recognize the stationery."

"I'll read the note to you."

Joan grabbed a pencil to take the message down in shorthand.

"Please call Joan Richards at 555-6223," the note began. "Dearest Sweetheart, I cannot live with my head; and with Social Security for the kids, I'm worth more dead than alive. All my love, Tim."

Well, at least that cleared up some of the questions she had. Her husband had not taken his action *against* her or the children. He had not wanted to hurt them in any way. Somehow in his illness he had made his tragic decision as an act of love. In his mind he had given all he could to help his family.

Apparently he had expected someone to discover him before the family arrived, since his note asked whoever found him to call Joan at her office. Joan shuddered at the thought of what would have happened if she and the children had discovered his body. She could imagine Mark tearing toward the house to see his daddy—and seeing his body by the car.

Again Joan's heart lifted in praise to God. In the midst of overwhelming sorrow God had once more showed His love and watchcare over her and the children.

Leaving the funeral home, Joan went to make the arrangements with the welfare agency for the funeral. It would be pushing things a little to get the approval needed before Thursday night. She would have to keep moving.

On Thursday, Tim's father flew in. Joan had not received any blame from him when he visited his son in the hospital, but she couldn't help wondering how he would feel about her now. Would he hold Tim's

125

death against her in some way?

His hug when she met him went a long way toward reassuring her. Later he remarked, "I just wish I'd been more honest with you before you ever married him, Joan. I knew way back then, but I hoped for the best, I guess. He never was right after those convulsions he had when he was little."

"Convulsions? What convulsions? I never knew Tim had convulsions."

"He started having them when he was 4, and the doctors couldn't get them controlled for anything."

"How long did this go on?" she questioned.

"For about two years. He'd have a convulsion every week or two. We never did find out what caused them, but they finally stopped."

Tim's father would never understand fully the relief she felt from that conversation. Nothing she had done after their marriage had led to her husband's illness. His dad had recognized its existence long before that. She certainly didn't hold it against him for hoping for the best—any parent would have done the same.

That afternoon food began to arrive. Joan was in the process of transferring her membership from one church to another, but it was neither her old congregation nor the new one that performed the thoughtful service. She barely knew anyone in the two small churches near her, but those virtual strangers rallied to her support. Joan would always feel a special warmth to those saints who knew what it meant to give.

Later she slipped away to talk with the parents of the child who had discovered her husband's body. "Is Joey OK?" she wanted to know.

126

"Yes, I don't believe the experience really hurt him," the father said. "It certainly shocked him at the moment, but he's fine."

"I'm glad it was not my own children who found him when we came home," she whispered. "I'm not sure they would have survived that."

"No, that would have been rough. Joey seems fine, though, and I don't believe he suffered any permanent damage."

Joan was thankful for that. She realized that if she and the children had arrived home on time the evening of Tim's death, they would have been there before the ambulance crew picked up his body. She knew God had spared her children one more shock.

Tim's brother, Carl, arrived just in time for the funeral. "Joan, I don't know how you did it. You stood by and supported him in ways none of the rest of us could have."

Relief again! Apparently none of Tim's family intended to place any blame on her. "Thank You, Lord, for that," she whispered. "It certainly makes things easier."

At last the service ended. Since the burial would take place privately next day, the family would escape its agony. To further spare the children, Joan had asked that the casket remain closed during the service. She knew that anything dead especially horrified Janet.

Joan had allowed each of the children to handle the grief of losing their father in the way that seemed most comfortable. Allen continued to attend school, never missing a day. The others only wanted to stay near Joan, perhaps afraid to let her out of their sight for fear something might happen to her, too.

127

At the funeral Debi and Kathi, half hysterical, kept stiffling giggles. Joan understood they were only using them instead of tears to release the terrible sorrow they felt. After the funeral they left immediately with Laurie and grandma. They needed to get away for a few days.

The friend who had sold Tim his car came up to offer Joan his sympathy. "I'm so sorry! I tried to help him by letting him have the car. I had no idea he'd use it to take his own life."

"Of course not. None of us could know. I only appreciate your efforts to help. You stood by as a friend all the way through. No one could ask for more." Joan had appreciated his support so much she almost felt she needed to offer sympathy to him.

"Is there anything I can do to help?" he wanted to know.

"There is one thing you could do," Joan replied. "Could you get that car out of there? Right now it hurts to see it, and I can't get it started."

"Of course. I'll be over this evening as soon as I can change," he assured her.

The whole family breathed a sigh of relief to have the vehicle gone. Its presence had continually reminded them of the pain.

That night Joan found yet another text that brought comfort. Psalm 68:5 says, "A father of the fatherless, and a judge of the widows, is God in his holy habitation." Her children were not really fatherless after all. God was their father in a special way now, as well as being the one who would stand by her.

Chapter 13

Guilty?

Friday Joan had another job to do—clean out Tim's apartment. Possibly she would be able to get a few dollars back on the cleaning deposit and rent. She spent most of the day getting all of his things packed and the apartment scrubbed spotless.

As she worked, Joan found so many things that made her think of happier times—a picture of the children when they were little, the wall plaque she had given Tim that Christmas they were engaged, a letter she had written him years before when they had to be apart for a short time. Everything she touched spoke of the one she had promised to "love until death do us part."

Now death had parted them, but her love had not died. Would she ever see Tim again? Joan didn't know. She had grown up with the conservative idea that someone who committed suicide was lost. Was the concept really Biblical? Joan wondered.

That evening she went through the messages received at the funeral. One read, "I guess poor Tim was just too lonely and depressed to be able to survive without you." It brought other questions to her attention: Was Tim's death in some way her fault? Would he perhaps be alive yet if she had let him return home?

If she caused his death by her actions, wouldn't that make her guilty of murder? Furthermore, if Tim were spiritually lost because he committed suicide, wouldn't she be guilty of far worse than murder? To take a man's life on earth is terrible, but to destroy his chances of eternal life is impossible even to consider.

Too much to cope with now, Joan pushed the problems away to read a bedtime story to the children. She felt thankful God had provided a day of rest. At least on Sabbath she would have a few hours when she didn't have to work. But she could think. The questions that bothered her would no longer permit her to ignore them.

Who was responsible for Tim's death? Joan felt a little paranoid herself as friends either avoided the subject or gave her a hearty "Don't feel guilty. You know God can forgive anything."

If I need God's forgiveness, then I must be guilty of something, Joan reasoned. Oh, I've certainly made mistakes. There's no question about that. But murder?

One friend, perhaps feeling responsible himself because he had not been able to help Tim enough to prevent his suicide, said, "We need to be so careful of what we say and do. We just never know when something we say might cause someone to make a decision like that."

Well intentioned as his remarks were, they only drove the feelings of guilt deeper into her mind. She remembered again the sympathy card that suggested Tim had committed suicide because she wouldn't let him come home. If she had refused to listen to the doctor, would Tim still be alive? Or might some greater tragedy have taken place, with the whole family perhaps killed?

Round and round her thoughts flew. Where was the answer? Did the roots of a problem like Tim's lie in childhood insecurities? If so, then why do some people from terrible homes come through strong, while others from good home backgrounds sometimes turn to suicide? Many times even children from the same home react in totally opposite ways to virtually the same situation.

She claimed a Biblical promise she had known for many years: "If any of you lack wisdom . . ." Suddenly a part of the text she had never noticed before leaped out at her: "and upbraideth not." Did God really mean He wouldn't say, "It's your own fault. You got yourself into the problem—you'll have to get yourself out of it?"

She looked up James 1:5 in her Bible. It actually said, "If any of you lack wisdom, let him ask of God, that giveth to all men liberally, *and upbraideth not;* and it shall be given him."

"Lord," Joan prayed, "please help me to understand. Thank You for showing me that You won't leave me to solve my problems by myself, but will help me to understand better."

The answer came not as a sudden insight, but little by little she came to comprehend better God's plan for humanity.

Joan knew that husbands often carry a burden of guilt for their wives' decisions, and wives for their husbands'. Probably the largest group of guilty people are parents. Parents generally feel it is their fault if their children make wrong choices. Even children are ashamed if parents do something out of the way. And a child involved in a parent's suicide is certainly in over his head as he tries to carry a burden on his young shoulders that he can't even understand.

Yet Galatians 6:2 tells us to "bear ye one another's burdens." Doesn't that mean, she asked herself, we are responsible to some degree for the actions and problems of others? Somehow there must be limits to what God wants us to bear for one another.

The more she studied and prayed, the more she realized God never intended anyone to be responsible for someone else's decisions, only for his or her own influence. The only burden we can carry for others is to pray for them and do our best to help them.

One girl Joan knew had spent many years as a drug addict because of guilt. As a 15-year-old she had become upset and screamed at her father, "I hate you! I wish you were dead!"

Two days later he took his own life.

Did her temper tantrum cause her father's death? Actually, her father had just gotten the news that he had inoperable cancer. To spare his family needless grief and expense, he had chosen to end his own life. But all Joan's friend thought of was her own loss of self-control.

A death of any kind, particularly a suicide, tends to make people wonder what they could have done differently—and that means guilt.

Laurie mentioned the story of Judas. He was a

constant companion of Jesus for three and one-half years. Shouldn't Christ have been able to prevent his suicide?

Of course, Joan told herself, but God will never compel the will. Then something clicked into place. God wouldn't force Judas to choose eternal life, but she was feeling guilty because she had not been able to make Tim choose rightly.

Finally Joan came to the understanding that no action of ours, either good or bad, can *cause* anyone to take his own life. In taking on the guilt of Tim's suicide, Joan assumed a burden Christ Himself did not bear with regard to Judas' death! If He could not prevent Judas' suicide, how could she think that she could have stopped her husband's?

Problems and sorrow seem to offer good excuses for some to take their own lives, but if mounting pressures caused suicide, then who would be alive? Joan knew she would certainly have opted that way out. No one is immune from tragedy, yet not all choose suicide. Why?

Apparently, freedom of choice makes the difference. Some might decide on suicide when everything looks great, while others live through great trial and never consider the possibility. Outward circumstances, then, do not determine the choice made. It is a decision made deep inside a person, and is really only between him and God.

Joan's friends who tried to help never intended to hurt. They didn't know what to say because they had never been through the experience themselves.

When one of the children asked, "Will we see daddy in heaven?" Joan faced the other big question that bothered her.

She really didn't know the answer, so she quoted what the pastor had said at the funeral: "God will decide." But somehow that wasn't enough. She felt that was only a cop-out for the real answer: "No, daddy committed suicide, so he can't be saved."

Someone remarked, "Since Tim was mentally ill the last year of his life, he wasn't really responsible for his own actions. God will take all that into account."

Joan wondered whether that really excused him before God. Does God have a plea available in His court "Not guilty by reason of insanity"? Besides, what caused his illness? Wouldn't that have to enter the picture too? If something over which he had no control produced his condition, then the answer would seem quite simple. God would discount anything done during Tim's sickness. But if, on the other hand, wrong choices he had made himself caused it, then God would surely have to judge differently.

"It's the trend of the life that counts, not the occasional good or bad deed," another friend observed.

But Tim's life had ended in suicide. Didn't that mean a downward trend?

Again Laurie came to the rescue. "Have you ever thought of the story of Samson? You know he committed suicide, yet Hebrews 11:32 mentions his name as being among the saved."

Joan began to study. Nowhere did she find any indication that anyone was spiritually lost *because* of suicide. King Saul and Judas were lost, but the Bible record indicates it was because they had turned away from God, rejected Him and His leadership, not because of how they had ended their life.

In reading Samson's biography in Judges 13 to 16, Joan discovered little good in his life. After failing God repeatedly in many ways, Samson finally turned to Him again as a blind slave. Responding to his prayer, God even gave him the special strength he needed to end his own life along with the lives of thousands of the Philistines. He had turned a seeming failure and suicide into triumph and victory.

Gradually Joan began to see that God would take much more into account than just the manner of Tim's death—or even the good and bad deeds of his life.

Motive seemed to be at least one factor. No marriage would even remain together, for example, if the partners did good things only from duty, not out of love. Yet it is easy to forgive many mistakes when others perform them in love (even if it is mistaken love).

If motive is the big thing, Joan thought, what about Tim's? According to his note, one reason behind his suicide was to help the family, but the other was because he didn't like himself. Were human motives ever a pure strand of good or bad? And did not God recognize and deal with that fact?

As she considered what she knew of Tim, one minute she would decide that God would surely save him because of his motivation—and then she would think of something else and feel He couldn't after all.

Joan realized it was an area she could not fully understand this side of heaven. All she knew was that God would judge her husband with a love much greater even than her own. It was love that saw everything in its best light.

Peace returned to her as she gave the question of Tim's salvation into God's hands, where it belonged. Only when she could let go of her burden of guilt and trust God to judge Tim was she free to accept the happiness He was waiting to bestow on her.

Chapter 14

My Father's House

Janet was crying so hard her mother couldn't understand what she was trying to say. Finally Debi came on the phone to explain the problem.

"Mom, on the way home from school today Janet's shoes fell apart." Debi was upset too. "What are we going to do?"

The children knew that Joan couldn't do much about the problem that night. But even though it was only a few days before payday, she simply wouldn't have *any* money left over for such luxuries as shoes.

It was now six months after Tim's death, and the family's financial crisis continued unrelentingly. The first thing Joan did each month was return to God what was rightfully His. Then she stretched every dollar three ways to make ends meet. With God's help she had managed to keep three meals on the table each day, as well as provide the clothes the children needed.

The two days Joan had planned to have off from work for packing had stretched into three, two for funeral arrangements and one to clean out Tim's apartment. Unfortunately, she had not made much headway in packing—and on Sunday, Joan still had to move according to plan.

Saturday night she and the children got a little more done, and Joan continued working alone far into the night. Then Sunday morning friends rallied around to help her with the actual move. One showed up with a truck, and others came to help with the heavy lifting.

Ready or not, the Richards family moved on schedule.

Monday and Tuesday, Joan spent cleaning. Again friends joined in to help. By Wednesday, when she returned to work, she could say she was *out* of the old house, even if she wasn't exactly settled into the new.

Gradually things had begun to return to a routine. The children could walk to school at last. Joan was now the only member of the Richards family who still had to commute.

The tight finances were the only thing that refused to settle down. She still found it nearly impossible to make it from one month to the next on her salary.

Right after Tim's death Joan had gone to the nursing home where he had worked to see whether they would let her have his final check. The extra seventy dollars certainly helped that month.

Then she contacted the apartment manager where Tim had stayed to see whether she could get a refund on the cleaning deposit and unused rent. Since Joan had had to pay for both when Tim first took the apartment, she felt she was especially entitled to that money.

"I'll have to check the records," the manager told

her. "We'll send it to you by mail if we find we do owe you something."

Wait again!

When Joan didn't hear from him in a reasonable time, she contacted him again. "What have you found out? Have you checked the records yet?"

"Oh, yes, Mrs. Richards. As a matter of fact, I did. Actually, your husband owed us money, since the apartment was vacated without notice. You did get the apartment nice and clean, but we've still lost money on it. I'm afraid we don't owe you anything."

Joan could hardly believe her ears. The man actually thought Tim owed him money, since he had not given notice! But since there didn't seem to be much she could do short of going to court, she decided not to try to collect. It wasn't worth a court battle.

Meanwhile she had contacted Social Security to see what she needed to do to get support for the children. The clerk told her she would need birth certificates for each of the children, and explained further, "Your benefits will be based on what your husband earned during the last ten years."

"This past year he didn't earn much," Joan replied, "since he had a nervous breakdown a year ago."

"Was he able to work during the past year?"

"A little. Just enough so he couldn't claim disability."

"Did he hold any job for as long as three months?" the clerk persisted.

"No, eight weeks is the longest he ever worked at one time this past year."

"Then he would qualify for disability payments

for the past year. Of course, you'll also be able to collect death benefits."

Joan had not expected to receive any kind of disability benefits, so that came as a pleasant surprise. God always came through with more than she deserved.

The clerk explained that it would take about three months for any of the money to come through, but when the payments began, they would be retroactive to the time when Tim first became ill.

All Joan had to do was wait. Again!

Joan had had to find a new baby-sitter for Mark when the family moved. She recognized as church members a couple shopping at the grocery store one day just before the move. So they started chatting. After a few minutes she asked whether they knew anyone who might take care of the boy.

"I don't take in baby-sitting as a rule," the woman replied, "but I have a little boy about Mark's age, and I'd be glad to do it. The two boys can go to kindergarten together."

Although Joan thought she was looking for a baby-sitter, she got more than she asked for. Mark found a substitute dad. The father arrived home each evening about an hour before Joan did, so he'd use the time to work and play with the two little boys.

Once he took both boys out of school for the day so they could work with him in the woods, gathering firewood. Many times when Mark's "other family" went camping, they'd include Mark and any of the other children in his family who wanted to go.

Again God had blessed beyond Joan's understanding. He had known and supplied her needs before she even knew she had them herself.

Allen and Debi seemed to suffer most from changing schools. Over and over as the year passed, Joan would have to comfort first one and then the other.

"Nobody likes me. I don't have any friends. *Please,* can't we go back to our old school?" They knew they couldn't, but they missed their friends intensely.

Finally, about halfway through the year, they began to make friends. At last the tears began to dry and the smiles reappeared.

Although Janet's pediatrician still insisted she should stay on medication to control seizures, Joan could see that the drug was hurting her. Weighing the damage she could see from the medication against possible harm from another convulsion, Joan decided to take her off the medicine.

She kept it available, planning to give it to Janet if she were sick. The girl had no convulsions. Gradually Janet became more alert in school, and much easier to live with.

When Joan explained the child's history to her new pediatrician, he nodded. "I agree with what you've done. I have a son with similar problems. You have to decide what seems best based on what you see in the child's behavior. Just keep her medicine handy in case she does get sick. She's doing fine."

About the same time the date arrived for Joan to go to court to adopt Allen and Janet. After a long road from foster care to adoption, they at last were really hers. God had answered again and again the prayers she had sent up for His help.

But still no Social Security benefits came through. Joan kept checking each month. The office finally said they would put the case through as a hardship situation.

By now six months had passed since Tim's death—and still nothing. Joan was worried as she hung up the phone after talking with the children about Janet's shoes.

"What can I do, Lord?" she prayed. "You've promised to supply our needs, and You always have. Now Janet needs shoes. She can't go to school tomorrow without them, and I don't have the money to buy them."

As usual she felt better after taking her problems to her Friend.

A few moments later the phone rang again. "I forgot to tell you we got some mail," Debi said.

"What did we get?"

"Well, there's something in a funny brown envelope that says 'Social Security.'"

Normally Joan didn't let the children open her mail, but now she asked the girl to open the letter.

Debi dissolved in tears.

"What is it, honey?" Joan urged. "What's wrong?"

"Nothing's wrong, Mom," she sobbed. "This is a check for $2,213.14."

God had known the condition of Janet's shoes long before her mother did. "Before they call, I will answer" (Isa. 65:24). He had answered before Joan even knew what to pray for.

That evening a happy family went shopping. They bought items that they had long gone without, with exclamations of "The check came the *same* day the shoes fell apart, Mom."

The Richards family knew they would receive regular payments from now on. The long night was over. With Social Security now coming through, Joan would be able to buy the house she was living in. It would be good to own instead of having to rent.

Joan had always disliked paying bills, but now she found it downright exciting. She went back to each company that had accepted the 50 percent settlement from her—and paid the other half. It was fun to go to a store with the money to pay a bill she didn't have to. Always she asked for the same person who had made the settlement with her in the first place.

A few companies told her they had no way of accepting the money, since they had written off the account, but many had kept the file open in the hope that Tim might someday recover enough to settle his half. None could have come back on her to collect.

Joan shared what God had done for her with each person she contacted. One man who had been raised in her church said wistfully, "I should never have left. I only wish I had the faith you have."

Another told her his wife was a member of her church, and he felt he would like to know a God like Joan's better.

Mrs. Lindstrom, of Fashion House, was almost as pleased as Joan was. "I knew God could see you through. I'm so glad you had the faith to work it all through with Him."

Joan expressed her own appreciation. "I don't think I would ever have had the courage to try if it hadn't been for your encouragement. God certainly used you to help me when I needed it most."

About two years later Joan obtained a job only a mile from home, which ended the long hours of commuting. Besides, now she could be available when the children needed her. Again God was good.

"Mom," one of the them asked, "will we have to go through anything bad in the time of trouble, since we've already been through this?"

"Well, I believe things may be easier, because we've learned a little about trusting God," she replied.

Joan knew their past experience would not change future events, but the habit of trusting God would make problems seem smaller. She felt no fear of the future because she had God by her side. Things would not always be easy, but "all things work together for good to them that love God" is still true (Rom. 8:28).

Now she felt that if God could take her safely through the problems of the past, she could surely trust Him to finish what He had begun. "We have nothing to fear for the future, except as we shall forget the way the Lord has led us, and His teaching in our past history."—*Life Sketches*, p. 196.

She didn't intend to forget. She knew now a few of God's "thousand ways."